ESSENTIAL PRESENTATION SKILLS

Speaking to Inform, Inspire, and Invite

by

Rosemarie Barnes

Spotlight PUBLISHING

Goodyear, AZ

Essential Presentation Skills – Speaking to Inform, Inspire, and Invite
Copyright © 2020 by Rosemarie Barnes

ISBN: 978-1-7345325-0-0

Cover design: Angie Analya
Interior design: Becky Norwood and Kandie Kunz
Published by Spotlight Publishing™ - https://SpotlightPublishing.Pro

Rosemarie Barnes - International Speaker
International #1 Best-Selling Author
Executive Presentation Trainer
www.confidentstages.com
rbarnes@confidentstages.com
250-661-0994

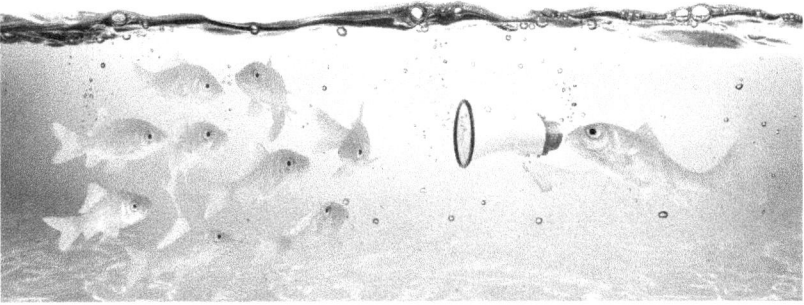

ESSENTIAL PRESENTATION SKILLS

Speaking to Inform, Inspire, and Invite

By

Rosemarie Barnes

Rosemarie Barnes

CONTENTS

Rosemarie Barnes

Chapter 1

Confident Intention

Confident Intention

Why do we speak in public? There are many reasons, of course, the most usual being to:

- ✓ Inform
- ✓ Inspire
- ✓ Motivate (no, inspire and motivate are not the same thing)
- ✓ Persuade (no, motivate and persuade are not the same thing)
- ✓ Educate
- ✓ Invite, and of course,
- ✓ Sell

All speakers strive to inform, inspire, and invite some sort of reaction or participation but the nuances of speaker intention make a massive difference to how the message is received. All require slightly different approaches in order to engage the listeners.

Different audiences have different needs and it is up to the speaker to fill those needs.

Speaking to Inform

When the purpose of the presentation is solely to inform, the listener is not guided to any particular response. Just as we see on a news broadcast, the speaker is simply reporting; there is no judgment, positive or negative from the speaker, but just the facts as they are known at the time. There is no expectation of listener action, and the speaker is not asking for a response; the only purpose is to share information.

Speaking to Inspire

When speaking to inspire, the audience is craving, "more." They want their passion to be ignited. They want to be guided by example, so they can see that they can reach higher, go farther, go faster, accomplish more, serve humanity better. They are looking for something more than where they are. They are seeking a more accomplished role model, or a higher purpose and they want to know that achieving it is possible. Think Martin Luther King's "I Have a Dream" speech.

Speaking to Motivate

A perfect example of motivational speaking is the coach of the losing team at halftime in the game. To motivate is to add energy into reaching a goal, in this case, to win the game. The speaker changes the atmosphere in the space by energizing and electrifying the listeners to try harder and assures them that with this increased energy and focus, a positive end result is not only possible, but will be hugely gratifying. The purpose of a motivational presentation is to spur the listener to action.

Rosemarie Barnes

Speaking to Persuade

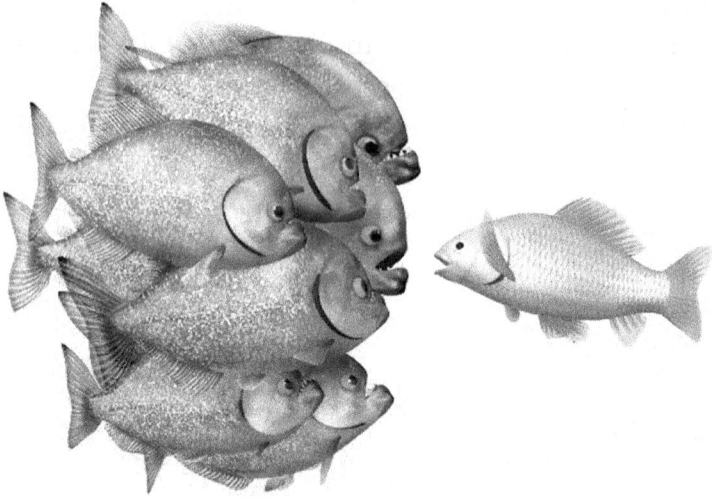

To persuade is to convince someone to amend their point of view to match that of the speaker. Speaking to Sell contains some of the same strategies as Speaking to Persuade, but the intention is different. The most difficult of all the intentions, persuasion is a gentle art: push too hard and the listener will react negatively, push too little, and they will not see the benefits clearly and possibly not react at all. Think of a criminal lawyer convincing the client to make a deal instead of risking the consequences of losing the case altogether.

Speaking to Educate

Very different from speaking to inform, the speaker's task is to provide a means for new information to be accepted and internalized as life-long knowledge. In this intention, the speaker must engage right-brain and left-brain thinkers as well as at least the 3 major learning styles: auditory, visual, and kinetic. Information must be explained (auditory), illustrated (visual), and exercises or other kinetic opportunities provided for learners to test, prove, and ultimately accept the information as truth.

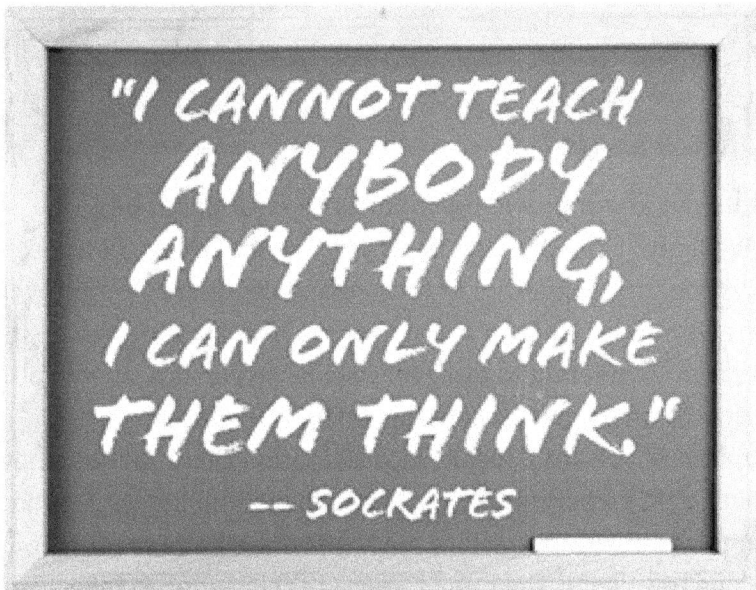

"I CANNOT TEACH ANYBODY ANYTHING, I CAN ONLY MAKE THEM THINK."
-- SOCRATES

Speaking to Invite

Invitation is about providing opportunities for continued involvement. It can precede or follow information, inspiration, motivation, or persuasion, or it can stand completely on its own. Asking someone out for a social evening is an invitation that stands on its own. A meeting to discover mutual interests is an invitation that stands on its own. It contains no hint of obligation or commitment toward a result. A presentation that outlines a new product is an invitation to investigate its possibilities by meeting again to get down to specifics. Very often used as a precursor for speaking to sell, it is the hook to tempt the listener to take a small taste, and it is created to make them want the entire meal.

Speaking to Sell

The intention of speaking to sell is to convince the listener to open their wallet and purchase your product or service. Every word spoken is intentionally chosen to nudge the listener to the inevitable conclusion that making the purchase is good for them, their business, their cause. The speaker with this intention highlights the positives of making a said purchase and validates the cost of the purchase to match the needs and solve the problems of the listeners. Scarcity and urgency are peppered either overtly or subtly throughout the presentation such that the listener feels compelled to act immediately and in their own best interests.

All excellent speakers know their intention and the result they want **before** they begin to create their presentation.

All excellent speakers use bits and pieces of each of the Intention strategies to engage every member of their audience.

All excellent speakers know the top of mind problems and questions of their listeners and weave the answers to those problems and questions throughout their presentations. If we don't know what those questions and problems are, **we find out**, again, before we begin to create; if we don't know what they want or need, how can we hope to speak directly into their hearts and minds?

Time is not the friend of any presenter, so using it to best advantage is paramount; spending time speaking about theories of social consciousness is pointless if the listeners' top of mind problem is poor employee engagement or increasing cash flow; even if social consciousness will increase employee buy-in or ultimately improve cash flow, for the presentation to be successful, speaker intention must be directly aimed at the spot that hurts the most: their top of mind problem. Only after that need has been satisfied will the benefits of, in this case, social consciousness, be heard.

EXERCISE

The first part of this exercise is going to require a partner, and a wish to have a bit of fun. The second part will take a bit of work, but what you learn will be worth the effort. It is the fundamental first step in creating any excellent presentation.

Part 1:   Improvised Preparation and Learning

1. Find a trusted, fun-loving individual to "play" with.
2. Come up with a ridiculous topic for debate. For example, the value of mosquitoes.
3. One of you will speak on behalf of the mosquitoes, and the other will speak to the negative.
4. Choose your intention from the list of the 7 possibilities discussed earlier.
5. You already know the top of mind problem of your "opponent" courtesy of deciding which of you is speaking for the positive and which is addressing the negative. Make some assumptions about what some of the specific "sore spots" your counterpart will offer.

6. Take turns debating by allowing each other 1-minute intervals to make a point or respond to something the other has said.
7. Be ridiculous. Arguments must be logical but need not be bound by reality in its "earthly" sense. Use your imagination as to the massively vital role mosquitoes fill, or the horrendous tragedies they might cause. All your comments and responses must be phrased to fulfil your intention.
8. Continue until you are out of new comments to make, until the debate comes to a natural conclusion, or until you can no longer catch your breath from laughing.

Part 2: Focus and Practice

1. Select your favourite topic.
2. Define your audience. Be specific. Why are they coming to hear you speak? What do they need? What is in the way of them getting it? What line of work are they in: generally, specifically? What is their average age? What is their experience: Beginner, intermediate or extensive?
3. Define your call to action. What one single thing (one, as in less than 2) do you want them to do immediately?
4. Define how your topic will be of interest to them, and how it will benefit them.
5. Choose one of the 7 intentions listed and create a short (10-15 minute-ish) presentation to reach that intention AND answer their top of mind problem at the same time.
6. Choose a different intention, and tweak that same presentation, for that same audience, the same top of mind problem but with this new end result in mind.
7. Choose yet another intention and repeat #6.

You will notice the ease you feel with some intentions versus the discomfort you find with others. This is because we all have a natural predilection for the style of presentations. Consider why one is more difficult than the other and understand that all have great value. The more you practice adjusting your presentations to meet different intentions, the easier it will become and the more tools you will have at the ready within your speaker's toolkit. This toolkit will provide the skills you need when your audience is not engaging with you as wish them to, or when your research on their needs turns out to be less than accurate; simply change your intention on the fly, and reach them another way.

By keeping your intention clear, you will notice how the same information can be transmitted in different ways and with different words. Knowing your intention will keep you from going off on time-sucking tangents that, while probably fascinating, will not benefit you or your listeners. Combining audience needs with your intention is the essential technique for reaching their hearts and minds in a truly authentic and focused way, and ultimately leading all present to conclude that you are, in fact, an excellent presenter.

CONFIDENT STAGES

Rosemarie Barnes

Chapter 2

Confident Audience Focus

CONFIDENT AUDIENCE FOCUS

When you are in business with every word you speak you are giving a presentation. Regardless of the setting, regardless of the number of people in the room, or whether you are even in a room when you talk you are representing your business, your mandate, and your values. The only time you are not representing is within the walls of your home. Even then, your family is watching and listening; what you say and do will influence them today or tomorrow.

The impact of the words you speak depends on who is listening, the words you choose, how you say them, and so many more things that it can make you dizzy just thinking about it; small wonder the majority of people would rather do anything other than speaking in public!

Consider these possible scenarios:

SPEAK TO INSPIRE

Scenario 1: You have landed an important contract and production schedules are tight. One of your suppliers is not delivering on schedule so you arrange a meeting to discuss the situation. You are speaking to inspire.

SPEAK TO LEAD

Scenario 2: Your business is growing. You've hired 2 new team members and now the previously supportive work culture has begun to fray. You call a meeting to iron out some of the challenges. You are speaking to lead.

SPEAK TO INFORM

Scenario 3: You are an expert in your field and have been asked to deliver a presentation at a conference of your peers. You've been given 45 minutes to share with an audience of 500 attendees. You are speaking to inform.

SPEAK TO SELL

Scenario 4: You have developed a brand-new widget and are introducing the new product. You are speaking to sell.

SPEAK TO EDUCATE

Scenario 5: Systems changes are required that will necessitate some procedure adjustments. You call a staff meeting to discuss the impacts with your team. You are speaking to educate.

Although each of the sample scenarios has a defined purpose, all require a toolkit full of expertise; there are elements of speaking to inform, inspire, educate, sell, and lead in each of them.

Some of these situations are in-house, some are external. Some are one to one, others are one to a few, and still, another is one to many. Topics are varied, situations are varied, outcomes are variable. All present challenges.

What each of these scenarios (and a never-ending list of others) have in common is that in all cases, your goal is to engage your audience to listen, to consider, and ultimately, to accept your recommendations and point of view. You are in the position of power and control and the most important person in the room. Right?

Well yes, and no.

The truth of the matter is that sharing our thoughts, opinions, and brilliance takes a back seat to the most major mandate of communication excellence which is to

Answer the Listeners' Top of Mind Question

and

Solve their Top of Mind Problem

The job of the presenter is not just to give voice to their own thoughts but to speak them directly into the hearts and minds of the listener.

Let me say that again: it is not enough to simply present your own position. From the front of the room, from behind the desk, from across the boardroom table, or even kneecap to kneecap, presenters must realize they are not the most important person in the room. Most presenters make that mistake because when they are speaking, they are the center of attention. After all, the speaker has the information, done all the work, and is the one taking all the risks.

No, no, no, no, no.

The most important person is the one whose problem is being addressed, the one who has the most to gain or lose by hearing your presentation, even the more casual listener becoming newly acquainted with the topic.

Consider, if we, the presenter, fail to engage our listeners, does it matter how much information we share? If we cannot maintain that engagement, and listener attention wanders, what good is our eloquence, our advanced knowledge, or our recommendations?

If a tree falls in the forest and there is no one around to hear it, does it make a sound?

If a presentation is given and no one can understand it, does anyone benefit?

The point is that people listen from their own point of view. We all have personal and business biases, and we listen through those filters. The most powerful filters are:

What does this mean to me?

How does this make me feel?

How does this affect me?

Notice they are all focused inwardly. It is only after the listeners assess the presentation's possible effects on them personally that they consider its' effects on others, even those on our teams.

A coach announces the starting lineup. If a player is chosen, they may feel relieved to have made it, elated with the feeling of success, and excited to move forward. They celebrate! They are not concerned yet about transportation to and from games, getting their uniforms, or how the extra training will impact the rest of their lives.

Most importantly for our purposes here, rarely do the successful players give any thought as to how the coach came to the decision, what all the considerations were, or how difficult the process was. They certainly don't care whether the coach is nervous about making the announcement or speaking in public!

What they care about is how the announcement affects them personally. They care about whether they get the information they need, and they care about getting their questions answered. In their minds, they are the most important person in the room.

And they're right.

The coach does not come out, thank everyone for coming, thank the institution for inviting him or her to coach, or complain that traffic was bad today, because, at this moment, **No One Cares!**

In scenario 1 with you not getting what you need on time, your supplier is most concerned about his schedule, not yours.

In Scenario 2 where office culture is changing, your team members are upset by the impact of the new hires, they are concerned about how it impacts them; they are not concerned that the situation is taking you away from other responsibilities.

Scenario 3 has you on a conference platform where the 500 individuals listening to you speak have no interest in how difficult it was to create the presentation.

Scenario 4 is about selling, and selling is about finding a need and then filling it. Their need, not yours.

In Scenario 5 you are addressing system changes. Changes of any kind are always a great source of angst. Your team needs to know that you care about how those changes will affect them. They want comfort, and they expect you to deliver it.

#1 PRIORITY

Create a Like, Know, Trust, and Respect Relationship
by
Addressing the Needs of the Listener

In each case, the speaker's #1 priority is to speak to the listeners' conceptions, misconceptions, and sticking points such that a Like, Know, Trust, and Respect relationship may take seed.

AUDIENCE FOCUSED LANGUAGE

The language we use has a great impact on the reaction of our listeners. Our society has become increasingly casual; women need no longer wear whale-bone corsets, and men have long ago given up top hats and spats in favor of baseball caps and sneakers. Our use of language has become similarly relaxed, and not always to our benefit.

For example, compare your reaction when a presenter addresses his/her listeners as, "you guys," versus, "Ladies and Gentlemen." The first is clearly more casual than the second and that's fine as long as it is appropriate within a group of peers. "You guys" can appear relaxed, friendly, and on equal footing. It can also be viewed as a sign of disrespect and it can lower your perceived expertise and intelligence.

"Ladies and Gentlemen," is more formal, more structured, and when delivered well, immediately tells the listeners that you respect them. Delivered less well it can be perceived as stuffy or pompous. Coulda, Woulda, Shoulda may be enough to wow some groups but definitely not others; it is up to the speaker to make a conscious decision about what language to use in order to best engage their listeners.

As always, it is not just the words, but their delivery that creates a reaction from the listeners. Erring on the more formal terms of address, respectfully spoken with warmth in the voice, open body language, and a sincere smile on the face will never get you into trouble. When you know your listeners well you can get away with a more casual demeanor and still have them actively engaged with you, but genuine respect and warmth are always received well.

Notice that the words and their delivery are audience-focused, not speaker focused. Show your listeners that you understand their situations and the Law of Reciprocity urges them to try and understand yours.

Some words are more powerful than others, especially when delivered with intention. The weakest word in the English language is, **I**, yet consider how often presenters begin with that word.

I

The strongest word is **YOU**.

Using you and we language instead of I and me, commanding your space, and truly respecting your listeners are fundamental to audience engagement.

AUDIENCE FOCUSED LEARNING

We all have our favorite way to learn, and there are many of them. As presenters, we consider the 3 most common learning styles:

- ✓ **AUDITORY**
- ✓ **VISUAL**
- ✓ **KINETIC**

AUDITORY LEARNERS

These are the individuals who learn best by hearing the information. They have a direct highway between their ears and their brain and sounds and words act as their file storage system. This is the way most teachers teach, and almost all professors, profess. These are the people that can easily get the information they need by listening. Anything else we provide for them (images, sound effects, exercises) are only enhancements for these learners.

VISUAL LEARNERS

Visual learners file information not through titles or words, but via images. The filing system for past learning is sorted by pictures. These individuals "see" information faster than they hear it. Seeing information laid out via a chart or diagram is more easily remembered than by listening to someone talk about it. Hearing information audibly or writing things down are only enhancements for this group.

KINETIC LEARNERS

This style of learning is grounded in movement. The movement doesn't have to be big, but muscle memory and brain memory have a direct line. The simple act of writing helps this group to transform information into knowledge. You will often find kinetic learners doodling while they are listening. This learning style is the most reliable for retention. They still benefit through audio and visual presentations, but for this group, the doing is the focus.

Excellent presenters appeal to all 3 learning styles: auditory, visual, and kinetic.

AUDITORY LEARNING

For the first, the Auditory Learners, it's a no-brainer. We talk, they listen, that's it. No enhancements required. While it is the most commonly used approach, auditory learning is not the most effective means for presentations; it is simply the easiest to create. We stand, we talk, they listen. Unfortunately, this style of presentation has limited success because historically, we tend to forget almost 90% of what we hear.

VISUAL LEARNING

The second group, the Visual Learners, still benefit from hearing information, but to seal it away, what they need most are images. This is where PowerPoint, Precis, and other slide platforms are beneficial. Speakers jumped on this bandwagon so fast, and so completely, that today, many presenters can't imagine addressing anyone without their visual cues and clues. When used in combination with auditory learning strategies, remembering information becomes a bit easier with people able to recall about 50% of what we see.

KINETIC LEARNING

The third major learning style is Kinetic Learners. When this group hears rhythm, their bodies are moved to join in. "Doing" is the key to reaching them. They listen, they see, but to cement information away, they need to touch, to express, to engage. This group enjoys writing, having a conversation with an elbow partner, doing an exercise or conducting an experiment. Although more difficult to manage during presentations, it is well worth the extra effort; while we remember only a fraction of what we hear and about half of what we see, we remember almost 100% of what we do.

We cannot know how our listeners absorb information and few presenters even give it any consideration. Most speakers simply create their presentations in accordance with their own learning style.

But you are not Most Speakers. You are seeking excellence and know that the more deeply you can engage your listeners, the more everyone will benefit. Presenters that appeal to all three of the major learning styles will have a greater impact than those who do not.

EXERCISE

1. Choose one of your favorite hobbies or pastimes.

2. Write 5-7 sentences about it as follows:
   - Sentence 1: introduction
   - Sentence 2, 3: Explanation
   - Sentence 4,5: Illustration (story, description, example)
   - Sentence 6: Activity
   - Sentence 7: Closing/Call to Action

3. Read it aloud, record it, and listen to it. This is how auditory learners enjoy receiving information.

4. What image would enhance your message? It can be a few words on a slide (only a few words!), it could be a photograph, perhaps a symbol, it could be a collage of color, use your imagination. What it cannot be is complicated, difficult to see, or with opposing messages.

5. Tell (read) your paragraph again, this time with your image(s) in clear view. Does your image attract or detract from the information you are sharing? This is where visual learners anchor their filing system so distracting or complicated images can be worse than none at all for them.

6. Give your audience some sort of activity. You might supply a fill-in-the-blank form for efficient note-taking. You may prefer to have them converse with an elbow partner about their own experiences with your topic. You might have them debating the pros and cons of engaging in the hobby or pastime. What about asking them to share their thoughts with the group? Use your imagination. This is where Kinetic Learners thrive.

Every person on Earth is special and when they are listening to you present, they want to know that you see them as such. It doesn't matter if your audience is seasoned executives or kindergarten children, none of us want to be viewed as unimportant. Show your listeners that you see them, understand or are willing to understand their point of view by speaking directly to their top of mind problem and answering their top of mind questions. Give them your information, your opinions, or your recommendations in ways they can hear, see, and do, so it is accessible and permanent.

Make your presentation about them.

You will engage them, and both you and they will succeed.

CONFIDENT STAGES

Chapter 3

Confident Content

CONFIDENT CONTENT

Arguably the most important part of a presentation is content and its organization. All presenters understand this, and we strive to give as much value as we can to our listeners.

That's where the misunderstanding begins.

Bringing value to our listeners begins as a trickle, grows to a creek, then a river, then a flood from which no one can escape! How many times have you heard a speaker say something like, "I have so much to share in the time I have, so I'm going to talk fast."

No, no, no! Promise yourself right here and right now to never, ever go down that road!

We know our subject matter inside and out. In our brains, all the pieces fit together into an organized structure that may have taken years to develop. When we try to compress all those jewels of information into a 60 or even 90-minute presentation, we can very easily release a torrent that leaves our listeners at best, confused, and at worst, believing we are just terrible speakers.

Confused Minds

Do Nothing

Limit your content to offer

CLARITY

and promote

ACTION

Know it now and know it forever: Confused Minds Do Nothing.

Human beings are married to the number 3. There's a reason that as children we enjoyed The Three Bears, The Three Little Kittens, The Three Billy Goats Gruff. We can remember 3 items on a shopping list. When we do something well three times, we congratulate ourselves on having learned it brilliantly and forever.

We remember the first thing we hear because it engages our attention.

We remember the last thing we hear best because it continues to resonate.

We remember the middle thing because it may connect the first and the last, or because it's only 1 more thing, and we can remember just one more thing.

Add more than 1 thing between the first and last, and we risk forgetting either or both of them. Some of us try to squeeze in even more between the first and last, and that's just a waste of time for both speaker and audience. If you absolutely cannot reduce your content to 3 rememberable topics, then give yourself and your listeners a substantial break (like a lunch break) about half-way through to clear the mind. The rule is a maximum of 90 minutes without a break. If you must divide your presentation into 2 parts, be sure the second half is the shorter of the two.

Not even we, as speakers, can remember our content when we pack in too much, so we rely on our slides and our notes to keep us on track. It is right here and right now that I shall self-righteously stamp my foot and proclaim that all excellent presentations can stand on their own albeit delivered in the dark, without electricity, and without enhancements, and still demand full attention such that we may inform, inspire, and invite continued participation and buy-in. Full Stop.

The **speaker** is the presentation, not the slides, the soundtrack, or the written script. While valuable when used to enhance your message, slides, and sound, even easels and markers cannot and should not be necessary to deliver your content; you, as the presenter are responsible for making your message memorable, rememberable, and valuable, and the very best way to accomplish that, is to limit the content in accordance with the Law of 3.

I ask you this: if you, who know your content inside and out, cannot remember your presentation, how can an audience, new to your topic, possibly hear, absorb, accept, and act on your premises?

What's the solution? So glad you asked!

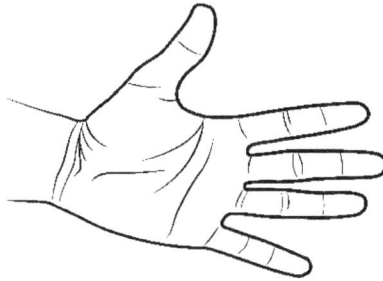

TALK TO THE HAND

The thing I love about this system is that we carry it with us: no fuss, no muss, no paper, no pencil.

Here's how it works:

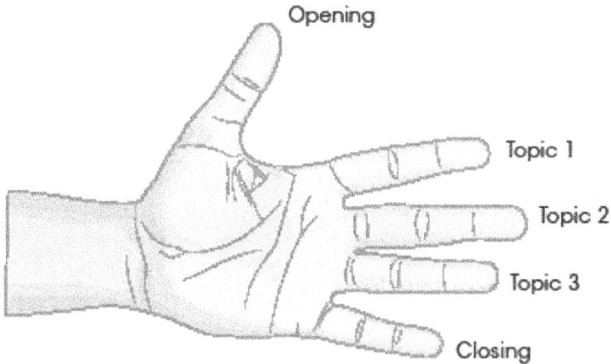

The thumb is the **Introduction**

Not to be confused with the host's introduction of you, (that you will always create for them, and which will include your credibility, experience, and expertise) your introduction of the topic must first be engaging and then command attention.

Never, ever, until you die, and maybe even later, does a speaker begin with announcing how glad they are to be there, or by thanking the organizers for inviting them. Of course, you are glad to be there, and you will have thanked the organizers long before you begin speaking. Time is not a speaker's friend, so do not waste it on banal and idle comments.

There are many ways to begin, my two favourite being either to ask an engaging question (one that cannot be answered by yes, or no), or by a bold, perhaps even marginally controversial statement. What you want to do is engage your listeners right from the first word you speak, and backing in slowly with non-focused comments will never accomplish that.

For example, a presentation about change could begin with,

"How do you react when a new system or process is imposed on you?" Please notice this cannot be answered by yes or no.

Alternately, "The world is changing faster than ever before. and we can either jump on the train or be run over by it."

Following the initial statement, and so that the listeners can know what to expect, the introduction then indicates what topics will be covered.

The index finger represents Topic 1

The middle finger represents Topic 2

The ring finger represents Topic 3

The baby finger represents your Closing and Call to Action

Confident Content

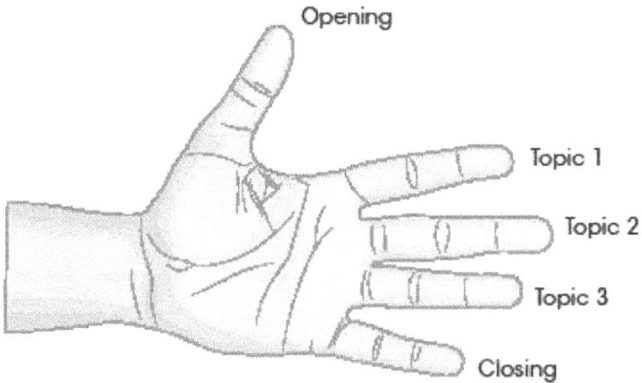

That's it. That's the basic structure of every excellent presentation.

If you are a visual learner, you may prefer to think of your presentation as a hamburger.

Looks delicious, but can you get your mouth around it? Can you eat it without making a mess? Can you taste each of the ingredients clearly? If this was a presentation, listeners would leave too full to be able to clearly remember individual aspects and decide what parts they prefer and which they would leave out. Instead of working so hard to distinguish each flavor and be able to reproduce it themselves, they will take the easier path and go with something simple, clearer, and easier to understand.

This burger, with its top and bottom bun (opening and closing), filled with the meat, tomato, and lettuce (topics 1, 2, 3) is much easier to digest, absorb, and use.

"But I have more to say than that!" we cry!

Of course, we have more to say than that, but the question is whether the listeners can absorb more that. Remember, that everything we say and do as presenters is for the listener's benefit, not our own!

When we have the luxury of ample time, we can expand the Talk to the Hand System to include up to 3 sub-points within each topic as long as we keep the structure very clear for the audience. (Hint: this is where enhancements are so useful.)

This is what it looks like:

Sub-topics and details give us an opportunity to expand our presentations while still allowing the Law of 3 to work for us.

I find this to be an excellent template to organize content:

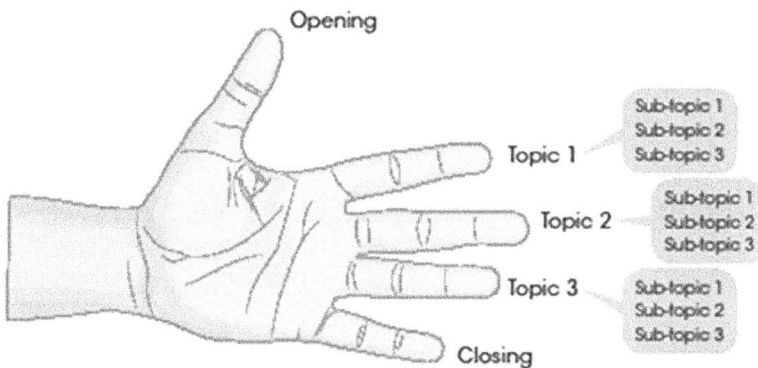

Presentation Template

	Opening	
	Topic 1	
	Topic 2	
	Topic 3	
	Closing & Call to Action	

Please notice the left and right columns are still empty, but not for long. This is where we post the amount of time allotted to each topic or sub-topic, and it is **very important, in order to fulfill the Universal Law of Professional Speakers:**

Thou Shalt NOT Go Overtime

Excellent presenters strive to end 5 or even 10 minutes early for 3 reasons:

1. Things always take longer than we budget for,
2. Spending too much time on Topics 1, 2, and 3, necessitates rushing through the final portion of the presentation. Speeding through the Closing and Call to Action does not allow us to make our overall message clear and will not incite our listeners to take action. Guaranteed. If our presentation is sales-oriented, we desperately need this time to make the final pitch. If we are speaking to inform, we will miss the all-important recap. If we are speaking to invite continued connections, the invitation will sound last-minute, and even perhaps a bit curt. Not good!

3. Audiences consider the extra few free minutes at the end of a presentation to be a gracious and courteous gift. It will certainly encourage the Like, Know, Trust, and Respect relationship to take root.

Presentation Template

	Opening	
	Topic 1	
	Topic 2	
	Topic 3	
	Closing & Call to Action	

The left-hand column of the template is where we indicate the passage of real-time, e.g. 12:15 pm-12:30 pm: Topic 1 or 2:30 pm-2:40 pm: Closing and Call to Action.

The right-hand column is for the number of minutes we will use to cover the topic, e.g. Topic 1: 15 minutes, Closing and Call to Action: 10 minutes.

Presentation Template

	Opening	
	Topic 1	
	Topic 2	
	Topic 3	
	Closing & Call to Action	

All of this structure is in aid of that universal law of presentations:

Thou Shalt NOT Go Overtime

Goodness! Did I say that twice? Yes, I did. Don't be surprised if it shows up elsewhere, too!

Diving a little deeper into presentation content and organization, and still paying attention to the Law of 3, let's talk a little bit about structure within each topic.

Each topic must contain the following elements:

	Topic 1:	
	Introduction:	
	Explanation:	
	Illustration:	
	Closing & Transition:	

Topic Introduction & Explanation

Just as our initial introduction commanded and directed attention to the entire presentation, so too, must the introduction to each of our topics. Once again, be sure to either state your case openly or garner attention by asking an engaging and thought-provoking question.

Remember that Topic 1 must arouse the curiosity or interest of the listeners and set the stage for mounting evidence to substantiate the closing and call to action of the entire presentation. This is where we begin to prove our worth to our listeners.

For example: If our purpose is to encourage participants to choose our widget over that of our competitors, then the introduction might look something like this:

"Our widget will not only solve your problem immediately, but it will outlast other solutions by up to 10 years."

We would then continue to explain the whys and ways of that statement, always emphasizing the benefits to the listeners.

Illustration

This is where enhancements can be valuable. An illustration can be an image, an example, a film clip, even a chart with very words on it (if you absolutely must). Best of all the possible illustrations is … Story.

Nothing is more enthralling than a good story. Whether it was a bedtime story when we were young, or a campfire story under the stars, or an Aesop's fable, stories get us involved by activating emotion. That's why the Rumor Mill is so active; rumors are primarily storytelling and gives us cause to react and emote upon the hearing of the tale and is often so juicy that we feel compelled to share the "news" with others. We love hearing and telling stories right from the time we are young to when we are fully ripe.

Stories ignite imagination and because they can take so many forms, give the speaker ample opportunity to involve not only our brains but our senses. A good well-told story will activate all the 5 senses: sight, sound, touch, taste, and the strongest one of all, smell. Once we involve the senses of the listeners, the vital aspects of Like and Trust become so much easier to attain.

Excellent presentations touch every one of our senses at least once and the use of story is the very best way to accomplish that. There are other very strong ways to turn information into learning, and learning to be internalized, and those will be discussed in detail in the Presentation Skills unit.

We may choose a story for one topic illustration, a bold image for another, an example or a testimonial for another; variety is not only the spice of life but the spice of presentations. The enemy of presentation excellence is monotony. Sameness. Predictability. Be sure to spice things up with as much variety as works for your topic.

Closing & Transition

The closing is where we make our point and underline it. We make the connections between our opening & explanation, the illustration, and the benefits and then we begin the essential task of transitioning from one point to the next.

Transitions are always the most difficult part, not only in presentations but in everything we do. In schools, for example, once the students are settled in and ready to learn, the teacher has little difficulty keeping them on task. It takes a few minutes for students to move from one classroom to another, a few more to meet and greet their elbow partners for the class, get out pencils and paper, share a story or two, and make plans for after school. When the class is nearing completion, the anticipation of the end can cause students to check-out before the learning is complete. In between, all goes according to plan. It is only at the edges that chaos and confusion find a way in. In the world of work, a portion of every Monday is spent chatting about the previous weekend, and on Fridays, our attention is split between work and the anticipation of playtime during the coming weekend. Tuesday, Wednesday, and Thursday are much more dedicated to tasks directly related to work.

We can control the ebbs and flows of listener attention by placing a good degree of importance on the transitions between topics. Remembering that a confused mind does nothing, connecting our topics for the audience is one of the very best ways we have to keep the audience engaged and open to attentive listening.

For example, if we are speaking about a solution for soaring recruitment costs, and if our topics are

1. Staff Turnover
2. Spiraling Retention Costs
3. Alternate Recruitment Methods

then the speaker must make the connections between them for the listeners by noting that increases in staff turnover (topic 1) has led to increases in retention costs (topic 2) and that they are now caught between a rock and a hard place. After going into a maximum of 3 details about those spiraling retention costs, the transition to alternate recruitment methods (topic 3, the most important of the three) may be framed as a plausible solution, and wouldn't that just be dandy for everyone!

We, the presenter, must never assume the listeners have made those connections, so we do it for them quickly and efficiently, and without belaboring the point beyond its usefulness.

If we bore them, we lose them.

Remember: if we bore them, we lose them so practice the transitions even more than the bulk of the presentation.

Now it's your turn.

Using the downloadable template, create the outline of a presentation.

Notice how it keeps your thoughts organized.

Notice how it keeps you from veering off on an interesting but not quite necessary tangent.

Notice how within the structure there is plenty of versatility and opportunity for your personality and style to shine, and,

Notice how the planning process becomes simple and functional, and above all, highly effective.

Once the outline and structure are complete, also notice how much easier the entire presentation is to remember, and how much more confidence you have in sharing your thoughts with your listeners.

The importance of limiting content to abide by the Law of 3, and of organizing that content into introduction & explanation, illustration, and closing & transition cannot be overstated, so, do yourself a good deed and practice, practice, practice until it becomes second nature. You will save yourself mountains of rewriting and frustration.

<u>Warning</u>

The Talk to the Hand System of content organization is

highly addictive to presenters

and may result in increased opportunities to

Speak to Engage and Speak to Succeed

Rosemarie Barnes

Chapter 4

Confident Presentation Enhancements

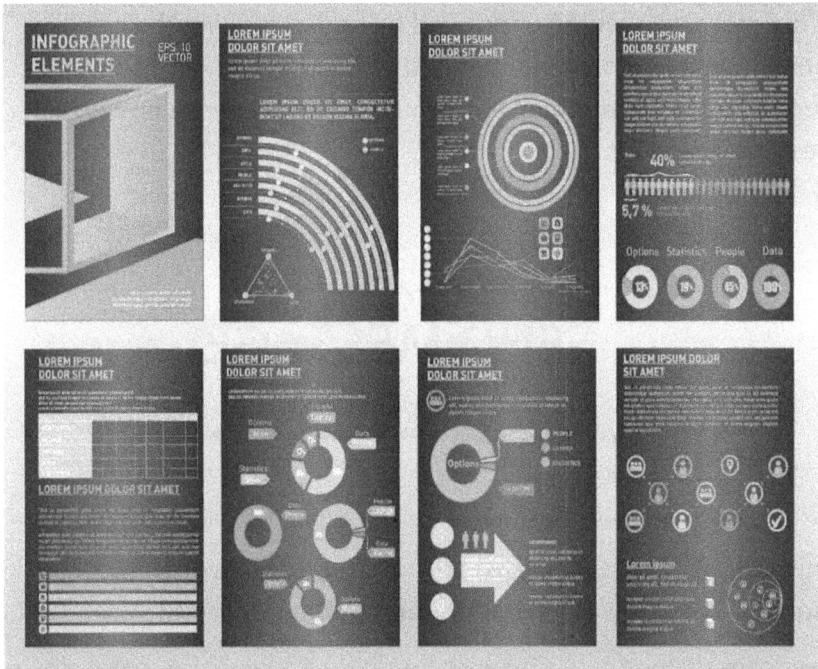

Confident Presentation Enhancements

Years ago, Dr. Albert Mehrabian was working with the FBI and Quantico to determine the best strategies for negotiations, specifically, how the messages we send are received by the listener. His work was groundbreaking for high-stress negotiations and was very quickly adopted by not only the best negotiators but by excellent public speakers as well. He determined that listeners receive information through the words they hear, the tone of the voice, and via body language. In and of itself, that wasn't much of an eye-opener but the percentages for each were surprising to many.

Dr. Mehrabian determined that although it was thought that most of the message would be received by understanding the words spoken, the results did not verify that idea. In fact, as it turns out, words are the **least** important vehicle for conveying a powerful message. Here it is then:

SEND MESSAGE

Only **7%** of the meaning is absorbed via the **words** the speaker chooses. We call that **Verbal Understanding.** Only 7%!

38% of the meaning comes from the speaker's **voice** or **Para-Verbal Understanding**

And a whopping **55%** of the message comes from the speaker's physical stature, posture, gestures, & movement, or the **Non-Verbal** cues.If over 50% of the message is delivered through our body language, and given that that absorption method is visual, then, your best visual aid is YOU.

YOUR BEST VISUAL AID IS YOURSELF

Be sure what you say, how you say it, and what you show, send the same message.

What you say, how you say it, and how you show it must be aligned to be believed. If the messages received by the listeners via words, tone, and body language are not aligned, it is the most powerful avenue, the 55% sent via body language that is taken to be the truth. Not the words, but the visual display performed by the body, yet scant few speakers give that element of their presentation more than a passing thought, if at all.

Inexperienced speakers can be intimidated and fearful of being the center of attention. At a subconscious level to make themselves feel less vulnerable they may attempt to hide by shielding themselves behind the lectern, and even more, by creating intricate and detailed slides. Once created, the speaker then uses those slides to keep themselves on track and confident. Some go even farther than that and simply read the verbiage from the slides to their listeners. When asked to create a presentation, many go straight to PowerPoint or Precis or any of the other slide-creation programs and use that as the basis for sharing their ideas. Little thought is given to vocal skills, delivery skills, or physical presentation skills as these speakers simply read aloud to the audience.

No, no, no, no, no!

NEVER, EVER, UNTIL YOU DIE, AND MAYBE LATER,

IS IT ACCEPTABLE

TO READ YOUR PRESENTATION TO AN AUDIENCE

It is **NEVER** acceptable to read a presentation or a speech to an audience.

Few public speakers are theatrically trained to be able to read aloud well enough to transmit thoughts and emotions much less connect with an audience while they are buried in their notes, and no one can do it with their backs turned while reading from the projector or television screen.

It is equally poor an idea to memorize your carefully chosen words and then recite them; the greatest fear of any speaker is that they are going to forget what they were going to say, and when adrenalin is already involved it is virtually guaranteed that a memorized script is the first thing to be forgotten.

A speaker's purpose is to make connections with their listeners, to solve their top of mind problem of the day, and finally, give them a solid course of action to follow. **None** of this can be accomplished when the speaker is reciting a memorized speech or reading aloud.

The hard truth is that YOU are the presentation, NOT your slides, and certainly not your notes.

PRESENTATION SLIDES

It is completely true that visual enhancements such as slides can be hugely powerful to underscore your words, especially because so many in your audiences fall into the category of Visual Learners who file their thoughts via picture; providing strong images creates solid anchor points for retention and recall. Unfortunately, so many speakers dilute their images with too many words and negate the impact of the picture itself.

Images can be extraordinarily powerful to the point where words are not necessary to explain their meaning. Not only can they enhance the meaning of your words, but they are also excellent for setting a mood and creating an atmosphere.

Consider the emotions that arise when you look at this image:

Compare that reaction to your response for this second image:

Were words necessary to cause a response to either image? Would explanations about the images enhance or detract from their effect?

Notice how the colors immediately tug on our emotions. Consider whether the striking blue eyes of the baby would be as pronounced or the mushroom cloud as powerful if different background colors were used. Take note of the way the images are cropped to bring attention to the message of the pictures.

Limiting the number of words on images is especially important when seeking an emotional response, and excellent speakers know the extraordinary power of emotion. Although facts and data are necessary to substantiate theory and processes, creating emotional connections and eliciting heartfelt responses is far more important.

It might be surprising to understand the care and attention excellent speakers use when creating or selecting images for their presentations, ESPECIALLY when we consider that technology tends to misbehave at the most inopportune times. Remember that your presentation must stand on its own merits even in the absence of working computers, the correct cables, or even electricity. It's almost ironic that even after we spend huge amounts of time searching for an image that perfectly enhances the meaning of our words, we, ourselves, the way we walk, stand, lean, gesture, and so on are so much more important than almost everything else that goes on upon the speaker platform.

To summarize the value of slides in a presentation:

1. Images elicit visceral responses far more quickly than do words.
2. Images are most powerful when verbiage is stringently limited; 0-4 words per image is ideal. Some speakers prefer a guideline of not more than 40 words over 10 slides. When additional information must accompany images, it is far

preferable to share it verbally than to have listeners read it from slides.

3. Never read information from slides aloud. Listeners can read silently faster than the speaker can read aloud so by the time the speaker is done the oral reading, the audience has long since finished and is making use of the extra time to check for telephone messages.
4. Reading slide information to a literate audience who are capable of reading it themselves splits their attention between the speaker and the slide; **never** give the audience the opportunity to move their focus away from you, the presenter.
5. Images assist all listeners to retain information, and most especially for visual learners.

You may be saying to yourself, "All this chit chat about limiting verbiage and statistics on slides is well and good for transformational keynote speakers, but how does that apply when the purpose of the presentation is to supply data for information, or when numbers, and costs, and overruns, and bottom-line numbers are singularly important?"

In these situations, you choose to supply hard copies (or easily accessible electronic copies) of the numbers/statistics/data for reference. Create the accompanying slide of the data and use moveable highlighting to focus attention on individual areas of interest or concern. Most importantly, and this cannot be over-stressed, your job as the speaker is not to read the slide aloud, but rather, to interpret the data and make it meaningful as it relates to addressing the listeners' top of mind problems/situations.

This is where the power of story comes into play, and there is **nothing** that can rival it for effectiveness as a presentation enhancement.

STORY AS A PRESENTATION ENHANCEMENT

Everyone loves a good story. and it doesn't matter whether the tale begins with, "Once upon a time," "In my day we had to trudge 5 miles to school uphill both ways," or "Did you hear what happened yesterday?"

It is difficult to resist the draw of a well-told story which accounts for the delight with which so many individuals participate in fueling the proverbial, "rumor mill;" relaying a juicy bit of gossip or even an interesting tidbit of news draws attention to the teller of the tale making them feel important, seen, and heard, even if the story has nothing to do with themselves.

In presentations, the use of story gives the speaker a direct, non-stop highway into the emotion center of the brain, while at the same time imparting valuable information. When a speaker inserts an example or illustration via story, their vocal tonality, speed, pacing, pausing, and enunciation change, sometimes quite dramatically.

Remembering that 38% of the meaning of the presentation is received via para-verbal (vocal finesse) means, this change of vocal timbre is, in and of itself, a powerful way of making the audience suddenly become tantalized to know what is to come next. When what comes next is a story and therefore, entertaining or at least thought-provoking, listener attention is guaranteed.

For speakers, the story is not always designed for entertainment. Rather, it can be used to show an example, illustrate a possibility, provide perspective, enhance meaning, and so on. The story need not be long to be effective; even a sentence or two delivered as an aside can provide an example or explanation. Story may be incorporated as a metaphor, may teach a lesson, may be serious or whimsical, yet will always garner increased attention on you, the speaker.

For some topics or situations, it may be more difficult to picture the use of story as a presentation enhancement, but it is exactly in these situations that its value is most powerful.

Consider for a moment that you are giving a presentation to share the latest data on health care costs to a group of left-brained, linear thinking, and bottom line-driven financial analysts. In the world of finance, these qualities are admirable, respected, and demanded. These are the individuals that can readily separate fact from emotion and who tend to make decisions based on statistics and empirical evidence.

Of what value is story to this audience?

In this case, story is used to humanize statistics. If the data indicates that one in three people will be afflicted by a severe illness such as cancer, stroke, heart attack, that number will be questioned or accepted as a mathematical average without much emotion attached. If, on the hand, the numbers are presented and then an example given via an aside comment or a more complete story, emotions will be activated, and stronger meaning attached to them.

For example:

"One in three people will get cancer, have a stroke, or suffer a heart attack. Look to your left. Look to your right. If those 2 people look healthy…."

Or

"One in three people will get cancer, have a stroke, or suffer a heart attack. When a close friend of mine got cancer, it was devastating to not only his family, but to his job, and subsequently, to his bank account. It cost him, it cost his family, and it cost his company."

Or

"One in three people will get cancer, have a stroke, or suffer a heart attack. Look around the room. Now imagine every third chair empty."

GUIDELINES FOR USING STORIES IN PRESENTATIONS

There are no hard and fast rules for the use of story in presentations, but there are some straight forward guidelines.

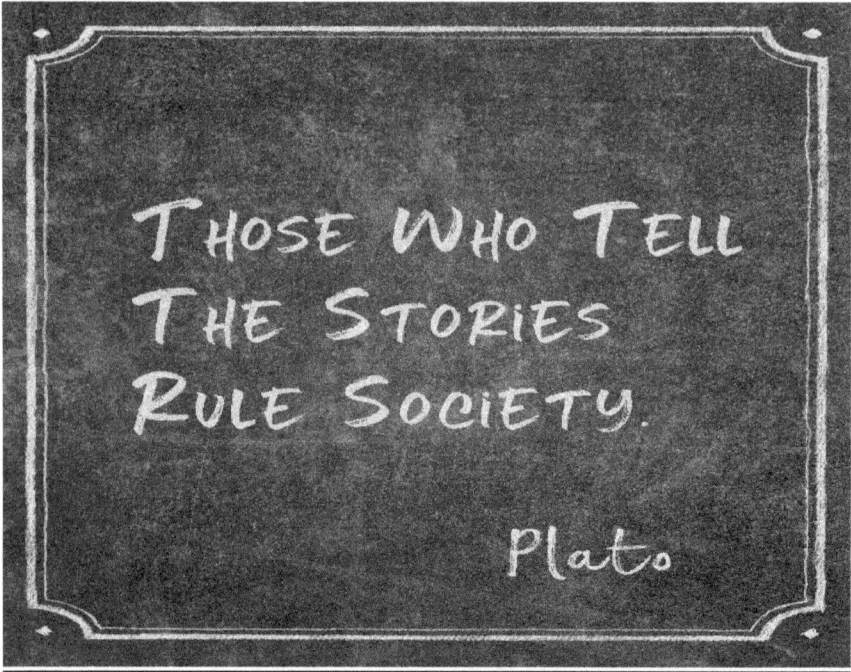

THOSE WHO TELL
THE STORIES
RULE SOCIETY.

Plato

The most powerful person in the world is the storyteller.

The storyteller sets the vision, values, and agenda

of an entire generation that is to come.

Confident Presentation Enhancements

1. Story may be used for example, illustration, or metaphorical purposes, its chief function is to activate the right-brain and elicit an emotional response. Remember that even for the most logical and stoic of us, emotion (right brain) is the basis for all decision-making, those decisions then backed up by rationalizations (left brain).

2. Story must not be self-indulgent. Remember that everything you say and do from the platform is for the benefit of the listener, not for yourself.

3. Stories must be fundamentally true but may be adapted or slightly modified to underscore its relevance for each audience. For example, if you are speaking to a room of women, it is prudent to have a female as the predominant character in the story.

4. Avoid **telling** in favor of **showing**. Instead of, "He said," and, "Then she said," speak in present tense actually playing the roles instead of using third-person narration.

5. Avoid being the hero of the story as it may seem boastful or attention-seeking. An example of someone else in the role of the "good guy" saving the speaker's skin is much stronger because it elicits a broader spectrum of emotions from listeners.

6. Provide only relevant details. Extraneous or unimportant details detract from the core message and may cause confusion as to the purpose of the story.

7. Presentation space is not the arena for self-therapy. Avoid tales of personal challenges from which you emerged only by the sweat of your brow, the lasting effects of which still

61

haunt you to this very day. No one cares. Your listener's primary concern is for their own struggles, not yours.

8. End every story by sharing what it has to do with the listeners. Do not ever assume they will correctly translate your example to their own situations.

MUSIC/VIDEO AS PRESENTATION ENHANCEMENTS

Music hath power to soothe the wild beast. It is an equally powerful tool to increase energy and encourage participation. Many speakers employ music before, during, and even after a presentation. Done well, music can create excitement, promote an appropriate atmosphere, and enhance receptivity. Done poorly, it can cause anxiety for both presenter and audience, create a distraction, foster irritation, and discourage acceptance.

Workshops are prime places for using music to bolster energy, and oftentimes catchy rhythms, well-known lyrics, and memorable melody lines are employed immediately after lunch when tummies are full, and brains are tired. Only a small amount of encouragement is necessary to have the audience up on their feet dancing by themselves or en masse. Some speakers even arrange for audience members to take their dancing to the platform as encouragement for others to join in the fun, thereby increasing blood flow to the entire body including the brain.

In the beginning, at breaks, and even in the end, music is an extraordinarily strong motivator. High energy music with strong rhythms motivates people to DO, so it is easy to see the benefits of piping in an urgent drum beat when asking an audience to sign on the dotted line. More sedate rhythms and smooth melody lines are used when the audience is asked to work individually using the information they have stored in their heads; slower tempi and richer melodies encourage audiences to THINK.

Music can also be irritating; much as I enjoy occasional bagpipe serenades, even for me, with a boundless appreciation for music of all genres and styles, a steady diet of the bass line drone of the pipes can make me want to make a bolt for freedom. Because music creates emotional responses faster and more completely than almost anything else, it can be a treacherous road to travel. Just because a particular genre, style, or even a single piece of music is your own perfect cup of tea, we must remember that not all people like tea.

Be mindful of the volume; blasting the audience out of their seats can activate the fight/flight response. On the other hand, if the volume is too low, it is a wasted effort. Also, be aware that not everyone hears well; too much sound drowns out conversation, while insufficient volume can cause anxiety over not being able to hear well enough.

Video is oftentimes employed as a credibility enhancer wherein the star of the show speaks well of the ideology, product, service, or speaker of the day. Because variety is not just the spice of life for a speaker, but rather an essential component of excellent public speaking, the different face and voice of the person(s) in the video is a brilliant mechanism to freshen up the presentation. A word of warning: videos must be short, they must be crystal clear both visually and auditorily, and they must NOT depend on a functioning Wi-Fi or other external electronic connection. The audience will not sit and wait quietly while we fuss and fidget to get the video to play; the phones will come out, sidebar conversations will begin, attention and energy will dissipate, and the speaker will have to exert considerable energy to bring it all back to the front of the room.

If you are fortunate enough to have someone running your technology for you, or if you are a whiz-kid at setting it up and are confident that your video(s) will play as anticipated, then, by all means, use them. When they work, they work very, very well at making powerful connections and providing great variety for your listeners.

FLIP CHARTS AS PRESENTATION ENHANCEMENTS

It is common to see speakers using paper/pencil/flipcharts/whiteboards as presentation enhancements. They are excellent for encouraging audience participation where audience thoughts are validated and rewarded via transcription to paper in full view of everyone present. Many who use this approach to visual enhancements will affix the flipchart pages to the walls as a reminder of what has already been covered during the presentation.

This approach works well with a few provisions:

1. Use bold colors for writing and consider the lighting in the room; some colors show up better under some lights than others. Orange, for example, cannot be seen well under regular fluorescent lighting, so be sure what you write can be seen.
2. Write legibly. There is no point in scribbles that remind no one of anything.
3. Remember the rule: turning your back to your listeners shuts them out of the conversation; poison to a public speaker.
4. Do not speak while you are writing. Ever.
5. Where possible, have someone else do the physical writing or drawing for you, while you continue to exercise control over the room and respect for your listeners. Make sure your scribe can write clearly and spell correctly!
6. Teach your scribe to leave some white space above, below, and around important points. White space magnifies the focal points by drawing attention to them.
7. Always repeat answers or suggestions from the audience. Not everyone will have heard them clearly, including your scribe.

While excellent speakers understand that their presentation must be strong enough to stand on its own merits and that they, themselves are the very best enhancement of their own words, we also understand that every audience will be composed of a variety of learning styles. Presentation enhancements assist us in connecting meaningfully with every single person present. We must consider and address the needs of the 3 most major learning styles of auditory, visual, and kinetic by speaking clearly and in the language of the listeners, by showing the meaning of our words through images, by giving examples and illustrations of those meanings via story, by creating atmosphere and motivation via music, adding variety via audio or video clips, and be rewarding audience participation by writing down their thoughts for all to see. We provide exercises and opportunities to absorb, to think, and to do, and we do it all for the benefit of those in attendance, not for ourselves.

CONFIDENT STAGES

Rosemarie Barnes

Chapter 5

Confident Presentation Impact

Confident Presentation Impact

You have a brilliant solution that will help solve the top of mind problem of your listeners. You have created content aligned with the Rule of Three and limited information to the amount your audience can absorb in one sitting. You have rehearsed and are confident you will not go over time. You have researched the demographics of your audience and are ready to speak their language so they can grasp concepts and details more easily. Your movement choreography is deliberate to assist **you** by engaging muscle memory and to enhance your message for your **listeners**. You have included experiential activities to enhance the absorption of meaning, and you understand how to control the room. The images you have chosen speak for themselves and contain only a few deliberate words. You have created a powerful closing and have a single, strong call to action to offer.

You are now ready to fine-tune the delivery for maximum presentation impact.

Entrances

There are many ways to make an entrance although often, they are dictated by the venue and seating arrangement. If you have the option, it is best to enter from Stage Right (your right as you are standing on the platform) because it assures the audience is comfortable. On the other hand, if you want to shake them up a bit, you may wish to come out strong from Stage Left; it has the element of surprise because, in the western world at least, we expect beginnings to come from the side from which we begin to read. You may choose to run up the center aisle with lots of energy. You may wish to be in full view while you are being introduced or appear only after its completion.

The real value of your entrance lies in your energy and that depends on your goal. It can be a bit tricky because what one person sees as energetic and strong, another may view as overbearing. Calm and gentle energy to one person may seem timid to another. Once again, the answer to the conundrum lies in knowing your audience, knowing what they need, and understanding how to communicate the solution to them. One simple remedy is to remember that you are there to serve your audience, and if it happens to benefit you as well, there's nothing you can do about that.

We all have a little helper we carry with us all the time. Although too much adrenalin will instigate the fight, flight, or freeze response, a little bit of excitement and perhaps even a wee bit of nervousness will add an irresistible sparkle to your voice, your eyes, your body language, your energy and ultimately, your message. A little bit of adrenaline acts like a beacon drawing people to like you, trust you, and admire you.

Introductions

Creating an impact begins long before you take to the speaker's spot. The venue, the atmosphere, the seating arrangements, the welcome your guests receive as they enter the space, all contribute to the way your presentation will be received. Not all of that is always within our control, but wherever possible, make decisions based on how you want the audience to feel and what you want them to do when they leave your presentation.

We can usually control or at least have input into the way we are introduced.

Always write your own introduction to be read aloud by the host. The host will appreciate your contribution because you are relieving them of that responsibility. In it, include who you are, what you are known for, credentials of concern to the specific audience, and any awards (if you have a lot of them, choose the ones that apply most to the topic of the day). Bringing up these assets yourself can feel like bragging, but the audience needs them to trust you know what you are talking about. Since it is not you delivering the introduction but rather the host, it will not appear boastful, but merely highly relevant. If you are not being introduced, give your audience that information on paper; it's easy to include it on the paper you provide for taking notes. Gracious hosts do whatever they can to make their guests comfortable and the experience valuable and pleasant. Since writing is a form of kinetic learning, why not avail yourself of another method for reaching all the learning styles? If the notepaper is branded with your information, it's a great way of keeping your name visible during the presentation. Whatever you do, do not deliver your own introduction about who you are, what you do, or why anyone should listen to you. Find another way to get that information to your listeners, and don't take up valuable presentation time with it.

If you feed them, they will come

… and so will the noise, the mess, allergies & preferences, and complications.

If you want someone to attend a meeting, promise them food; hence the doughnuts and muffins at office meetings. Although the promise of at least snacks may increase numbers in the audience, it is not always wise to provide it.

Addressing an audience while they are eating is **never** a good idea.

1. When we speak it is important to have full attention on us. Splitting attention between the speaker and the cheesecake means that parts of the message will be missed.
2. Serving staff asking whether you would prefer coffee or tea is similarly distracting, not only to the listeners but to the speaker.
3. Food is noisy. Whether is it the cutlery on the plates, the cellophane from the crackers, or the crunching reverberating in the audience's ears, it is all white noise and guaranteed to dilute the speaker's message.
4. Food that one person finds acceptable may be entirely unsuitable to another. Providing food means getting involved in dietary needs and restrictions, not to mention personal preference. No matter what you do, you will not please everyone. Ask yourself if you really want or need to go there.
5. Decide whether refreshments will enhance or detract from your presentation and go from there. Sometimes providing food is worth the extra headaches it will inevitably bring, but make it available before or after you speak. **Never** attempt to deliver a presentation while the group is actively consuming food.

Eye Contact

"At least he made eye contact this time."

Whether on stage or off, we all know that eye contact is the quickest and surest way to make connections with others; no eye contact, no trust; no trust, no deal.

One of the best reasons for greeting people as they enter the space is to make eye contact at the same time as shaking their hands and welcoming them in. Physically touching someone to shake their hands is a sign of trust. The shaking of hands is proof that no weapons are concealed, and no harm intended. Looking into the eyes is a sign of honesty, at least in western cultures and it is expected. If you are speaking in other parts of the world, it can be wholly inappropriate so be careful. Even the way we shake hands is different across the world and can be used to insinuate control or superiority.

It is not difficult to make eye contact in one to one situations. Not making eye contact is a signal that something is not right; distrust is always the result. Where there is a physical distance between the parties, as it is when a speaker is addressing a group, it can be a bit tricky to look someone in the eye. Having made that initial connection as a participant was walking in the door, the speaker needs only to send a glance their way to promote the feeling of recognition in both parties.

It may not be possible to meet and greet every person in attendance, so over the course of their presentation, speakers must strive to make eye contact with as many as possible. The question of how long to hold that contact can be a bit tricky: too short and the individual will not feel truly seen, too long and they will begin to feel uncomfortable as if they are being stared at. Watch their body language; it will tell you very clearly when they wish to break the connection. One or two seconds of held eye contact usually does the trick.

EXERCISE

You will need a partner. An acquaintance, colleague, friend, or relative will do.

Using the phrase, "I appreciate your input on that last project," experiment with and take note of the reactions of both of you as the phrase is delivered in the following scenarios:

-while looking at the ceiling
-while looking at the floor
-while looking just over their heads
-while looking at someone else
-while looking at their chin
-while looking directly into their eyes.

By noting your own and your partner's reactions, you will very quickly observe the emotions that accompany each. When you are speaking to a group, each member still wants to know that you are speaking **to** them, not **at** them, not around them, and not through them. It takes a bit of practice to perfect this skill (if perfection is even possible), but as with all things of true value, it is worth the effort.

By the way, understand that this skill is not reserved for public speakers but will benefit everyone, all the time.

Smiling

For eye contact to make the most impact, the facial expression must match the intention. Smiling sends a message of friendliness ... usually.

When the smile is sincere, the eyes close a bit, the outside edges of the eyebrows are drawn down, and the cheekbones rise up to meet them, the result being the laugh lines around the eyes. Real smiles can be the result or the cause of feeling happy. It's a package deal that releases traces of endorphins and dopamine, and it encourages others to join our emotional state.

However ... if the smile is insincere, it does not reach the eyes. it can look menacing, artificial, and does not invite further connection. It can also make us look slightly maniacal or unapproachable. Artificial smiles can utterly destroy trust and cause words to ring hollow and untrue. The lesson then is this: sincere smiles at appropriate times are always welcomed but if you can't trust the smile to be real, don't do it at all. Replace the artificial smile with a look of interest or respect, and it will be accepted as it was given.

Speech Pacing

Some people talk faster than do others. When we get excited or nervous, we speaker faster than we might otherwise do. No matter the speed, we can usually adjust to it and make meaning from the message provided that enunciation increases in proportion to the speed. Sadly, that doesn't always happen.

On the other hand, some people speak slowly. If the content is scintillating this slower pace provides an opportunity to hear, process, consider, and accept or reject the meaning. If the energy of the delivery remains high, we accept the slower pace. Sadly, that doesn't always happen either.

The term, "fast talker" is not a compliment. It denotes someone smarmy, underhanded, a trickster. Think about a commercial where the voice over is very fast and where the ending contains something along the lines of, "Not available in some stores. Some restrictions may apply." No matter how sincerely the statement is delivered, we are left with a sense of distrust. If a speaker were to give an entire presentation at this speed, we would be exhausted by the end of it and regardless of the content, would take little value from it.

The opposite of the fast talker is the snail. If the pace is too slow, we may become bored and amuse ourselves by checking for messages. Some individuals may find themselves in a constant state of déjà vu because we've reached the statement's conclusion and processed its meaning, judged its merits, taken out the trash, and waxed the car before the speaker finally gets around to conclude the thought. Once again, we are tired by the end of it and may take little value away with us.

These are, of course, extreme examples, and neither will propel you along your road to excellence.

In more moderate and realistic examples, there is nothing wrong with speaking quickly or slowly as long as it doesn't stay the same throughout the presentation. The secret to keeping listeners alert and engaged is variety. The same can be said of volume. Increased volume and speed can bring attention to a vital point, but for every up there must be a down; if everything is loud and fast, it loses its effect. Slow and low invites intimacy, but too much of that and the audience falls asleep.

EXERCISE

Record yourself telling a fairy tale with which you are quite familiar as if you were speaking to a rapt audience. Do not read or recite it. Feel free to insert the menacing voice of the big bad wolf, or the innocent voice of Little Red Riding Hood as the story demands. Tell the story from beginning to end. As you listen back to it, notice how the quality of your voice changes when relating just the narrative bits as compared to the parts with danger or intrigue. Pay attention to the variety of speeds with which you spoke the words and how the volume increased and decreased.

This is the power and wonder of the human voice and to not use a variety of intonation, speed, and expression is to deliver only a portion of your message.

Take particular notice of whether you are in the habit of dropping the ends of words or sentences and tossing them away as if they were not important. Perhaps you tend to conclude your thoughts by raising the pitch of your voice as if everything was a question. Neither habitual dropped nor question endings will do you any favors in the world of presentations. Using questions in presentations is powerful, but only if you are really asking a question and it is well worth the effort to get out of the habit of raising your vocal pitch at the ends of thoughts as a way to elicit an indication of understanding. Understand, too, that under-delivering the final words of a sentence is like giving someone a sandwich without the bottom slide of bread. Don't shy away from posing true and rhetorical questions, making bold statements. It is stronger to "show" than "tell" so when appropriate go right ahead and, "act" out conversations rather than reporting them via third-person narratives.

In case this message is not clear enough yet, here it is:

Variety is the spice of life

and the sauce of presentations.

Offer your guests more than just dry toast.

Verbal Pauses

With apologies to William Shatner and his portrayal of James T. Kirk aboard the starship, Enterprise, verbal pauses are profoundly powerful …. unless they are used to excess.

In a world full of printed signs, bigger is better; the bigger and more colorful the sign, the more noticeable the words. The problem is that when everything is big and bold, it ceases to impress and becomes just an ignorable blur. As any graphic artist will tell you, when the words on a sign are surrounded by some white space, the contrast makes them more noticeable, and therefore, more important.

Similarly, with public speaking, for important words or phrases to stand out and be clearly heard, the excellent public speaking will insert short pauses in front of and behind them.

Using the phrase, **"Let me remind you that it is never acceptable to be late for a meeting, especially one called by the president,"** first try running it all together, and then insert pauses for effect.

Similarly, inserting a pause after making a bold statement will increase its strength.

Use this phrase: **"Make no mistake: ... we are all in danger of losing our jobs. ..... unless we cut excess spending immediately,"** and again try it first without pauses, and then once again inserting one or two for best effect.

Inserting active pauses is beneficial in more ways than only for attention.

An active pause or pregnant pause is full of expectations. It is full of anticipation and energy and when used well, can encourage listeners to sit up on the edge of their seats. An inert pause is simply a gap of nothing. Well executed pauses give just a moment for the listeners to absorb information before being presented with more. As long as the speaker puts energy into the pause, it is an opportunity for him or her to take a deep breath, change an attitude, begin anew. In the world of music, it is said that the most beautiful music happens between the notes. In the world of public speaking, the most powerful messages happen between the words.

The overuse of pauses leads to Speaking in Sausages. This is where James T. Kirk provides an example.

Must ... get to the bridge and ... target that ship!

Can you hear the sausage links?

These ... tribbles will .... create a ... problem.

Artificial or empty pauses are only torn holes in a tapestry. They detract from the artistry and have no value. Worse than that, during a presentation they create the same negative effect as the fast talker, causing the speaker to be viewed with suspicion or at least as artificial.

Exits

A presentation is not completed until everyone in the audience has left the room.

So many times, speakers say their last words, indicate they are finished by saying, "Thank you," and then rush off the stage faster than being shot out of a rocket.

How rude!

When the presentation has had a great impact, listeners respond via applause. They are thanking the speaker for sharing wisdom, suggestions, a course of action and so on. They have received value and are showing their appreciation. If they are ignored, it is a bit of a slap on the face.

Consider how you feel when you offer someone a sincere compliment and they either ignore it or cast it aside by saying something that belittles your opinion. Are you likely to pay them a compliment again?

Learning to accept compliments is a learnable skill. It can feel awkward to simply accept the kind comment and just say thank you, but it is worth the effort to learn.

Try this:

EXERCISE

Working with a partner or two or three, take turns saying something nice to each other. One at a time, pay the person you are standing beside a sincere compliment by telling them you admire an article of clothing, a new haircut, the way they handled a difficult client, managed a project or anything else that is true.

That's the easy part.

The difficult part is not saying, "What? This old thing?" or, "I could have done it in my sleep," or any other negating comment. By downplaying the compliment, you are telling them you do not value their opinion, or care about what they think. It is insulting to the person giving the compliment and does you no good whatsoever.

Instead, simply say, "Thank you," or, "That's nice of you to say," or another phrase of simple acceptance. Sounds easy, but it's not and you won't realize how difficult it is until you've tried it.

When a speaker doesn't acknowledge the applause, he is clearly showing that he doesn't value the opinion of the audience, or care that they enjoyed or took value from the presentation, and that is just plain rude.

First of all, saying thank you at the end of a presentation has turned into the expected way of telling the audience we're finished. For goodness sake, if they can't tell you are finished, your closing and call to action need to be rewritten!

A far more elegant way to remove all doubt that you have concluded the presentation is to stand in neutral, pause for 1 or 2 seconds, take a small step backward, put your feet together, and bow your head slightly. Bow even more if you are comfortable doing so. The applause will begin. Stay in that humble stance long enough to silently say to yourself, "I was terrific," and then stand up with a sincere smile on your face. That's when you can say, "Thank you." They are, after all, telling you they appreciate you, so it is only courteous to offer thanks in return.

Once the applause begins to die back, that is the time to gather your notes and find your way out of the spotlight. Not before.

Thus endeth the rant on making a meaningful exit.

LEAD GENERATION

It amazes me how many speakers do not take advantage of opportunities for lead generation, and I'm not just talking about keynotes or workshops here. To be excellent a speaker must be completely present and involved in the here and now, but tomorrow always comes and there is always follow up to be completed. How can you follow up with participants if you do not have their contact information? There are new laws in place to prevent or at least reduce unwelcome emails, so we can't connect with people without their permission. If, however, participants have supplied you with an address of their own free will, we can freely and legally get in touch with them, at least until they ask us to stop.

How then do we get their information? Via Lead Generators and the possibilities are endless:

Session Feedback forms
Free gifts
Request for service forms
Attendance sheets
Newsletter sign-up sheets
Blog sign-up sheets
Complimentary consultations
Door prize business card draws

Anything that entails participants voluntarily providing their contact information is fair game as long as you follow through and provide the promised service or product. In the case of feedback forms, just by sending a message thanking them for their input is an opening to keep the connection going.

Make your branded forms or response cards impressive so they are respected. Little slips of paper or dog-eared foolscap are just as likely to be used as scrap paper or turned into some delightful origami figure, as they are to be completed for your purpose, but beautifully designed and presented forms are either respected and left alone or are completed with legible handwriting and placed in the receptacle you are so graciously provide.

An excellent presenter is professional, and that professionalism must be shown in every aspect of our work, including how we walk, talk, carry ourselves, and even how we are represented electronically or on paper. It is the greatest and most versatile tool we have to make the greatest impact for the benefit of not only our audiences but for ourselves.

Rosemarie Barnes

Chapter 6

Confident Presence & Charisma

Confident Presentation and Charisma

What is presence?

The dictionary denotative definition says:

The impressive manner or appearance of a person.
"Richard was not a big man but his presence was
overwhelming."
Synonyms: bearing, carriage, stance, deportment, attitude,
manner, guise, demeanor.

What is charisma?

Dictionary denotative definition:

Compelling attractiveness or charm that can inspire devotion
in others.
"She enchanted guests with her charisma."
Synonyms: charm, aura, personality, magnetism, mystique

What is confidence?

Dictionary denotative definition:

A feeling of self-assurance arising from one's appreciation of
one's own abilities or qualities.

"She's brimming with confidence."

Synonyms: self-assurance, belief in oneself, self-reliance,
boldness, courage

Connotative Definitions

- **Presence** is the ability to garner attention, to be magnetic, to broadcast without effort or attitude.

- **Charisma** is the art of holding that attention by making others feel good about themselves when they are with us.

- **Confidence** is the knowledge that no matter what obstacles arise, what complications ensue, that you have all the right tools in your tool kit to competently resolve them.

In the world of presentations, **P**resence is the ability to garner attention, to be magnetic, to broadcast without effort or attitude.

Charisma is the art of holding that attention by making others feel good about themselves when they are with us.

Confidence: This one has a variety of implied meanings but the one that is the truest is the knowledge that no matter what obstacles arise, what complications ensue, that you have all the right tools in your tool kit to competently resolve them.

Confidence is less about how many successes we've enjoyed than it is about our capability of overcoming the trouble spots along the way. J.T. McIntyre had it right when he said,

Confidence comes, not from always being right, but rather, from not fearing to be wrong.

J.T. McIntyre

Confidence comes not from always being right but rather, from not fearing to be wrong, and one of the biggest contributors to it is rooted in knowing and living your values.

Confident Presence then is your own belief that you can dial your magnetism or demeanor up or down to suit the situation, whatever that may be, all the while remaining true to your values.

Similarly, **Confident Charisma** is your own belief that regardless of how thorny another person may be, they will feel seen and heard when they are with you, even while you maintain your own personal values.

Unfortunately, even the connotative definitions do not tell us how to acquire Confident Presence or Charisma. Some people seem to have a natural abundance of one or both, while others display neither. As a speaker, we need to not only possess these skills but be able to control the quality and quantity of them to suit the circumstance. Happily, both skills are completely learnable.

PRESENCE

To aid your understanding of Presence, let's consider what it is **NOT.**

Presence is not arrogance, nor is it a display of an overblown ego. It need not be loud or demanding. Presence is not static, and it is not automatic. Presence is not self-indulgent or used as a tool for manipulation.

The following well-known story was quoted in <u>The Charisma Myth,</u> written by Olivia Fox Cabane:

MARILYN MONROE WANTED to prove a point. It was a sunny summer day in New York City, 1955. With a magazine editor and a photographer in tow, Marilyn walked down into Grand Central Terminal. Though it was the middle of a busy workday and the platform was packed with people, not a single person noticed her as she stood waiting for the subway. As the photographer's camera clicked, she boarded the train and rode along quietly in a corner of the car. Nobody recognized her.

Marilyn wanted to show that just by deciding to, she could be either glamorous Marilyn Monroe or plain Norma Jean Baker. On the subway, she was Norma Jean. But when she resurfaced onto the busy New York sidewalks, she decided to turn into Marilyn. She looked around and teasingly asked her photographer: "Do you want to see her?" There were no grand gestures—she just "fluffed up her hair, and struck a pose."

With this simple shift, she suddenly became magnetic. An aura of magic seemed to ripple out from her, and everything stopped. Time stood still, as did the people around her, who blinked in amazement as they suddenly recognized the star standing in their midst. In an instant Marilyn was engulfed by fans, and "it took several shoving, scary minutes" for the photographer to help her to escape the growing crowd.

Confident Presence is a skill that can be controlled and dialed up and down at will. It is energy, it is an intention, and it is powerful. It begins with the confidence to be seen in your own skin, overtly and completely, you. It grows with the understanding that you have value both to yourself and to others, and it is so magnetic that it draws others to you like a moth to a flame. It requires that you want to be seen, not for the sake of being noticed, but so you are available to others who may benefit from what you have to offer. It is walking into a room with warm and attractive energy and it is being able to control that energy by focusing on being of gracious service to those who need it.

EXERCISE

Conduct an experiment.

Next time you are out in public, even a grocery store or shopping mall, focus on creating a magnetic energy field around yourself. Be curious about those around you, in a non-creepy way, and simply observe their mannerisms. Be open to possibilities while remaining calm and secure that you are who are, and that's enough.

Set the intention of catching their eye and sharing a very brief moment of connection. You will be amazed at how energy will transfer between the two of you. Acknowledge them with a small, pleasant smile, and go on about your business. If you remain curious, you will notice yourself being boosted by the shared energy and will feel pleasant... accepted.

Now, up the ante a little bit by bringing that same magnetic energy into your place of work. These people presumably know you better than do strangers in a shopping mall and have seen you at your best and something less than that. Don't be surprised if you hear comments like, "You look great today," or, "Looks like you had a terrific weekend." Also, don't be surprised if someone asks you to join them at lunch or seeks you out to ask you a question.

There is a super-highway between wanting to be noticed and the way our bodies manifest that desire, so be careful to use your new-found power for good, not evil. Master villains can be just as magnetic as can the good guys, so let your honorable values guide you.

After you've amazed yourself and others with your suddenly expanded presence for long enough that it becomes automatic, start experimenting with how large you can make your bubble of magnetism. Again, the point is not to make yourself the center of attention (there are quite enough professional attention-seekers around) but rather to be seen. There are hugely different attitudes between demanding attention, (Notice me. Oh, notice me.) drawing attention, (Oh, look. John just walked in) and accepting attention, (Good to see you, too.)

Public speakers who can control their presence can control a room simply by being in it. If we want to be of service, if we want our ideas and plans to be accepted, if we want to get the deal signed, we need to be seen and heard. We can do that via bravado and volume, or we can learn to broadcast our presence and make them come to us.

CHARISMA

After we have drawn people to us via our large and welcoming presence, we need to have them stick around so that we can be of service, assist in solving their top of mind problem, or make the points we wish to make. This is where Charisma comes into play.

Charisma is the art of making others feel good about themselves while they are with us, only in the most sincere way. It does not include giving unsubstantiated compliments, oozing sweetness, or anything that could be misconstrued as, "sucking up."

Charismatic people make us feel seen, heard, and valued. In conversation with these individuals, we feel interesting and we feel uplifted. Nothing feels artificial since the charismatic person draws us into the conversation by showing real interest in us.

Charisma is being kind, but not sappy, interested but not prying, curious but not nosy. It is the art of asking questions and truly listening to the answers. It is the ability to quickly elicit trust. It is focused on the message the other person is sharing. Charisma is the absence of multi-tasking wherein we are thinking of responses while they are still talking or wondering how long this conversation is going to go on. It is being completely present with that individual at that moment.

A word of caution: many of us are unaccustomed to being the sole focus of attention and it can make us uncomfortable. Looking someone in the eye is good, staring, not as good. Closing the physical distance between yourself and the other person can invite a closer connection, or it can be just plain creepy. We all have a personal space boundary, and it varies depending on where and how we were raised, as well as individual preferences. I call it the Personal Bubble. It is the dividing line between close and too close, questions and interrogation, seeking attention and stalking. It changes depending on the situation and the person to whom you are speaking: the acceptable distance between 2 women is much closer than between 2 men, or between a man and a woman. It is also culture-dependent; denser populations have much smaller personal bubbles than do those accustomed to more space. The same holds true for topics of conversation. Personal details may not concern some individuals at all while other, more private individuals will clearly back away from the conversation or even the group.

Charismatic people can draw us out of our shells and our protective walls, which is why it is so important to always stay on high moral ground. We never want to encourage others to feel the personal equivalent of "Buyer's Remorse," by feeling uncomfortable the next day because they said more than they meant to do. Just as in sales, handling returns is tedious and often unpleasant, so if it looks like your talking partner is about to over-share, you may want to turn the conversation to a safer topic.

 Charismatic public speakers can make each member of an audience feel important. If the speaker's intent is to be of service and provide value to the listeners, then when combined with presence, the size of the group is of little consequence. We do not have a finite quantity of charisma, but rather, as our intention to improve our audiences' situations grows, so too does the encompassing charismatic quality.

Choose your message that will assist your listeners with their top of mind problem, determine your singular, strong call to action, understand the emotion with which you want your audience to leave, and keep them safe from emotional extremes. Show them your sincere interest by focusing much more on their needs than on your own, and you will have them hanging on your every word.

That is the power of Charisma.

We draw people to us with our presence, we keep them with us via charisma, and we offer them confidence in themselves by demonstrating our own.

CONFIDENTSTAGES

Chapter 7

Confident Vocal Delivery Skills

(Part I)

Confident Vocal Delivery Skills

Part I

(High, nasal, harsh) Have you ever heard anyone speak with a voice that made you shudder as with fingernails on a blackboard?

(Loud, strident) How about someone too loud or just plain irritating?

(Sickly sweet) How about sickly-sweet condescension?

(Breathy) How clear can the message be if the vocal quality is too airy?

(False pauses) Can you remain attentive when the speaker uses fake pauses for imagined emphasis?

(Fast) How about listening to Speedy Gonzales?

The purpose of any verbal communication is to transmit a message and the words we use are vital to accomplishing that. If, though, as Dr. Mehrabian discovered that words alone are responsible for only 7% of the message our listeners receive, and 55% via body language, that leaves 38%, or over 1/3 of our message being shared via what our voice does.

Enunciation, tone, speed, resonance, clarity, even the amount of air we use affects how our message lands on the listeners' ears. Our voices are finely tuned instruments and must be respected as such. Can you imagine a solo violinist leaving his violin to be buffeted by harsh winds, dryness, or acid rain? Of course not, yet speakers abuse their instruments regularly. Forced breathing, dehydration of the vocal mechanism, and coffee, lemon juice, wine and so on have the same effect on the voice as does a harsh environment on a Stradivarius. As beautiful as the sounds from a well-tuned musical instrument may be, they are but imitations of the scope and variety available from the human voice. Although we are not singing our messages to our audiences, the spoken word has just as many musical qualities through which we can persuade, argue, inspire, and reassure, if only we learn to listen to the sounds we make with educated ears.

A little bit of knowledge about the moving parts involved with speaking makes it much easier to understand how to control the sounds we make.

Vocal Production

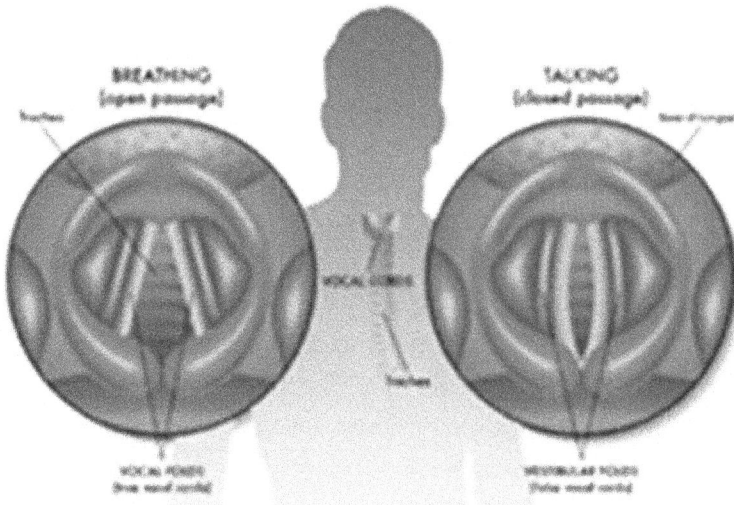

The vocal cords are located at the base of the throat. Although we refer to this piece of our anatomy as vocal cords, they are more correctly called Vocal Folds. Air passing over them causes them to vibrate, in turn, causing the air to vibrate thus producing sound waves. The quality of the ensuing sound depends on where the air is directed, and at what speed. The shape of the inside of our mouths, how we use our anatomical resonance chambers, the amount of energy in our cheeks, tongue, and lips, our posture, our hydration levels and tension all affect the quality of the sound. Steady vibrations can only occur with steady airflow, both in and out.

Let's first examine how breathing affects sound production.

Breathing for Speakers

Inhalation   Exhalation

The breathing apparatus includes the mouth and nose, the sinuses, the trachea, the lungs, and the diaphragm. Essentially, we inhale through our nose or mouth sending air down into the trachea, which leads to the lungs, which rest on the diaphragm. At rest, the diaphragm is shaped like a loose, inverted U, or an open umbrella. When we inhale, the lungs become inflated with air and require more room in the body, so the diaphragm flattens to accommodate. It takes energy to hold the diaphragm in that flattened state, and it is not that muscle's, "home base," so it naturally returns to its former domed shape, thus causing the exhalation and the unused or less useful component of carbon dioxide to be released from the body.

Posture

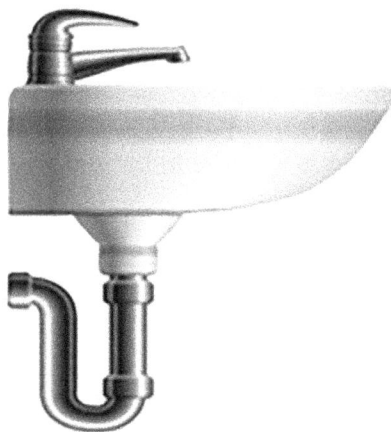

Using the visual of a bathroom sink, consider the basin to be your mouth and nose. The water (the air) enters the basin (your body) and is held in place (in our lungs) by the sink's plug (our diaphragm). Release the plug and the water can continue its journey down the pipe. Release the diaphragm and the air can continue its journey into and out of the body. If the drainpipe of the sink is crimped or bent, the movement of the water is constricted. If our trachea is crimped or bent via poor posture, the movement of our air is equally constrained. If you've ever had to lace up skates for yourself or someone else, or struggled to get a child into a snowsuit, you may have noticed that when you stand up, your face may be slightly red, and the urge to take a deep breath is irresistible. If you try to speak you will find your voice to be breathy and even ragged as the body brings itself back to normal breathing equilibrium.

Smooth and even sound waves depend on smooth and even movement of air. Ergo, good posture = controlled and reliable sound production; poor posture = erratic and unreliable sound production.

An equally important component of sound production lies within our resonators. Sound travels better through water than through air, which works out very well since 60% of the average human adult body is water; we are essentially walking, talking sound amplification units!

The resonating chambers we are concerned with here are in the sinuses.

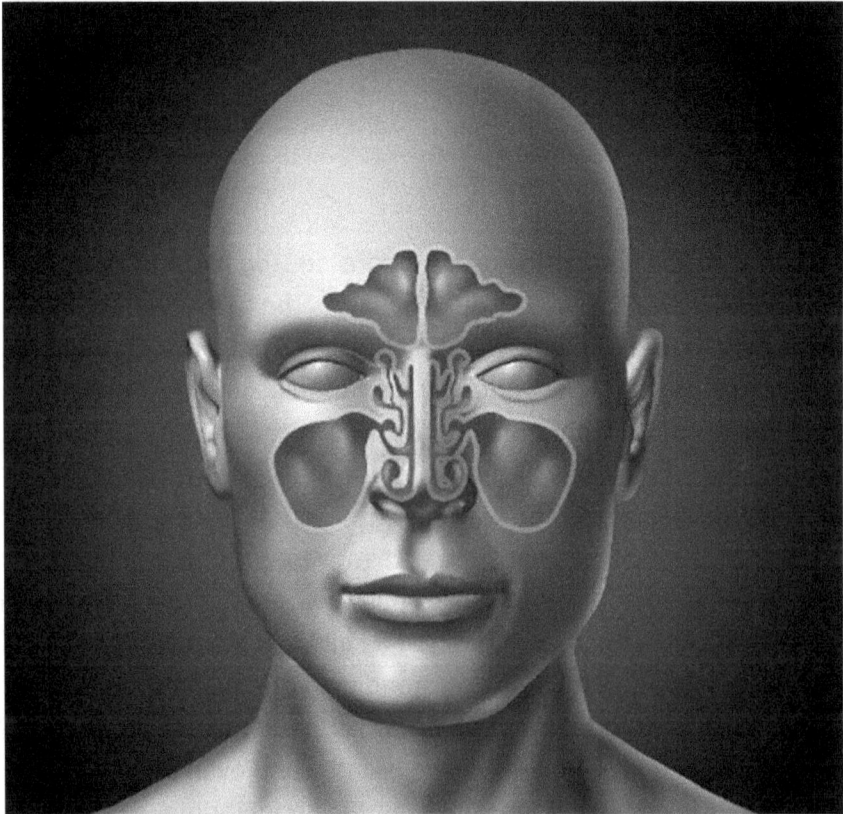

You can see the sinus cavities in the forehead, the nose, and the sides of the nose; these are the facial resonating chambers. We call it the Mask. The mouth and chest are the other major resonators for sound production.

When we hear sharply nasal tonalities, it is because the speaker is not allowing enough air into or out of the sinus cavities; the result is a thin sound that does not carry and is less than pleasant to hear much like a slightly out of tune cheap guitar might sound. When no air at all enters the sinuses, we <u>sound</u> as plugged up as we <u>feel</u> from a bad head cold. This condition even affects the pronunciation of some words as in, "I god a code in da dose." When we direct our air through the facial resonators, it is a light and nimble sound with tremendous carrying qualities.

The chest cavity is also a resonating chamber. The sound that is produced when engaging this chamber is (demonstrate) lower pitched, heavier, and sounds louder to us. Unfortunately, this resonance has little carrying quality, and the sound collapses very quickly after exiting the body.

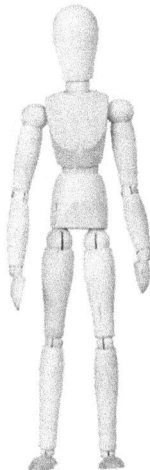

In order to control the quality of the voice and to direct the air into and out of the body, we absolutely must maintain good posture, that is to say, feet directly below the shoulders, weight distributed equally on both legs, knees, and hips aligned and not locked, torso straight, shoulders square, chest high, spine aligned, and head perched on top like the crowning glory it is.

Chest Breathing vs Belly Breathing

We can control how deeply we breathe.

Consider a sleeping infant. As they breathe, their entire torsos expand and release with each inhalation and exhalation. Each breath is slow, regular, relaxed, and deep. This is called **Belly Breathing.** If we are already at ease, it keeps us in that state; if we are tense, it can induce relaxation.

If we are startled, nervous, or suddenly called upon to act quickly and powerfully, adrenalin is released in the body giving us a burst of energy and strength. Our breathing immediately changes from low and slow to shallow and fast. Adrenalin coursing through our systems is what gives us the almost super-human strength and speed that allows the hero to rip the door off the burning car and save the child trapped within. As a race car requires increased fuel to zoom up to top speed very quickly, the fuel supply is equally quickly depleted, and pit stops are necessary to fill the tank and replace the tires. Similarly, under times of tension, our adrenalin supply is quickly used up, and we become fatigued. Our muscles, unused to extreme bursts of energy require pit stops to rest and recover. Our adrenalin supply is refueled more quickly than our muscles and brain can recover, and before the lactic acid from overused and strained muscles can drain from our systems. We can force our adrenal glands to work overtime to keep us going fast and strong, but with insufficient recovery time between episodes, we begin to suffer adrenal fatigue that eventually can result in mental and physical collapse.

Not good.

For most people, speaking in public is a nerve-wracking, adrenalin-fueled situation feared in about equal proportion to death itself. The comic, Jerry Seinfeld once said that if we must attend a funeral, most people would rather be in the casket than having to give the eulogy. This kind of stress causes an adrenal reaction which has both good and less good aspects. One of the most immediate symptoms is that we begin to chest breathe, the result of which is that what little air we are moving is directed away from the higher thinking functions of the brain and more directly into our muscles; we go straight into the survival mode of fight or flight which is brilliant if we are truly in danger, but not quite as good if we need to think clearly. You may have noticed that heroes who have just accomplished astonishing feats can rarely remember details of their experience; they will say things like, "I didn't think. I just reacted," and exactly what they did will be fuzzy at best.

As a public speaker, we must guard against allowing the release of adrenalin to deplete the oxygen supply to our brain. We have little need for feats of daring-do or athleticism while on the podium, but we do need our brains working at full throttle. Our number one defense mechanism against a full-blown release of adrenalin lies in our breathing. Keeping it low and slow, belly breathing keeps an over-abundance of adrenalin in check.

Our posture is a huge contributor to the ease with which we can accomplish this by clearing the air highway of twists, turns, and barriers.

EXERCISE

Stand in neutral, that is, straight, tall, proud, feet under shoulders, shoulders square, chest high and open.

Place your hands on your upper abdomen and take a few deep, slow breaths allowing your abdomen to expand and contract with each in- and exhalation.

Do not let your chest rise and fall, but only your abdomen. Close your eyes and notice how you begin to feel more relaxed. In and out, slowly, deeply, in and out. Good.

Now place your hands on the sides of your rib cage, about half-way between your armpits and waist. (If you are wearing a bra, it's right where the strap is.) Once again, take a few deep breaths, this time noticing how the rib cage expands and releases sideways. Repeat to the count of 10.

It is important to become comfortable with this sideways expansion because scant few of us are willing to let the front of our bellies expand and "hang out" while in front of an audience!

Now, check your posture to make sure you are still in neutral. Good.

This time, place your hand on your chest. Breathe so that ONLY your chest rises and falls with each breath. Do not let your abdomen move. Notice how the natural reaction is to breathe faster and inhale and exhale less air and how, after only a few seconds we feel a need to open our mouths. This is how we breathe when adrenalin has been released.

To illustrate the effect of chest breathing, and keeping your hand on your chest, pant like a dog on a hot summer's day. Open your mouth, let your tongue hang loosely, and take quick breaths while counting to 10.

Ready?

Go.

How do you feel? Do you feel the need to take a deep breath? Do you feel inclined, right now, to analyze a detailed spreadsheet of intricate numbers and data or do you need to take a minute to recover?

Is the inside of your mouth dry? How about your throat? Are you light-headed at all? Do you feel more refreshed or would you rather just sit down for a bit?

Controlling our air controls our adrenalin. While we do want a little bit of adrenalin in our systems such that our presentations sparkle with a bit of excitement, too much adrenalin causes us to think less clearly, speak less effectively, and be of far less value to our listeners. If, during the course of your presentation you find yourself at a loss for words and wondering what you are going to say next, take just a second to check your posture and your breathing. Take a low and slow breath and in just a second more, your memory and your poise will come back in full force, and on you will go with rejuvenated finesse and confidence.

When we go on to Part II of Vocal Production Skills, we will look at how to use and care for a public speaker's most essential tool: our voice.

CONFIDENT STAGES

Rosemarie Barnes

Chapter 8

Confident Vocal Delivery Skills

(Part II)

115

CONFIDENT VOCAL DELIVERY SKILLS

Part II

In Part I, we covered the mechanism for, and the importance of **breathing** for consistent, high-quality vocal production, and how good **posture** contributes to good breathing. We also looked at the effects of **adrenalin** and the way our breathing can reduce the chances of an overdose of this incredibly powerful hormone, thus keeping us clever and in control of ourselves.

Now we move on to the voice itself: the quality of it, the power of it, its weaknesses, and caring for it.

HEAD VOICE, MIXED VOICE, CHEST VOICE

Trained singers know of the 3 voices and use them to create the sound quality they desire. Speakers also benefit greatly by adding this knowledge to their tool kits. Consider an orchestra. The chest voice is represented in the bass lines; bassoons, double-basses, tubas, baritone saxophones, all low pitched and sonorous.

Chest voice takes advantage of the throat, lungs and surrounding areas for resonance. The head voice uses facial resonators. In the orchestra, this voice quality is represented by the flutes, the piccolos, the soprano saxophones, the violins. A mixed voice is just what you would expect; a combination of both. This is the cellos, the violas, the alto saxophones, the clarinets. It is not an either/or situation, and the percentage of head and chest voice in Mixed Voice can and should vary depending on the topic, attitude, and desired results.

And why? Because sound quality affects meaning.

EXERCISE

You will need a recording device (your cell phone will do just fine). Although it's not completely necessary, it's more fun if you have a partner, so see if you can round up one.

Use the phrase, **"We need to have a budget meeting."**

Before you speak the phrase, state the name of the emotion you are sharing about the words. For example:

Frustrated: We need to have a budget meeting. As a secret: We need to have a budget meeting.

Take note of your partner's reactions as you speak the phrase in different ways. If you don't have a partner, try to listen to the replay of your recording as if someone else were doing the speaking.

Deliver the phrase, "We need to have a budget meeting," as you would in the following circumstances and remembering to state the intention or associated emotion before you begin each one:

- In a noisy restaurant
- In a very hot environment
- In a very cold environment
- With frustration
- As a secret
- As if good news, and while smiling
- As if bad news, and while frowning

- As a command
- As a question

As you listen to yourself, the ensuing recording and/or your partner, can you hear the differences in the resulting tonality, speed of delivery, intensity, and breathiness? Can you hear how the voice automatically responds to our thoughts and intentions?

The range of volume in the human voice varies from person to person, and some people have louder voices than others. Some individuals have voices that are calming and sedentary, while others are sparkling and full of expression. All of us have a range of vocal pitch, quality, and volume that is as individual as we are, and all of us can extend our reach via learning and practice.

As long as our vocal mechanism is healthy, our voices respond to our energy levels, moods, and intention. Very low energy results in flat and expressionless speech, and vice versa. I'm sure you've heard excitable people telling a tale and noticed how they speak faster and faster, and how their pitch goes higher and higher. Others speak low and slow, and still, others are in between.

The thing to remember about your voice is that you are the only one that has it. Your voice is unique, and since we create the sounds we make internally, it is also very personal; comments made about voice quality can be taken as high praise or damning insult, so tread lightly.

Variety is key.

Let me say that again: the most important aspect of vocal production is the ability to provide a variety of pitches, of tone, of speed, of pacing, of pauses. Second to that is to match vocal expression with facial expression and with a physical expression so the messages are aligned.

EXERCISE

Prepare yourself. We are going to be exploring the vocal range, and you can expect to be making some weird and wonderful sounds. It will feel a little silly, and it is meant to such that a) you can enjoy the sounds you will make, and b) you will stretch your pitch range in a comfortable way.

Again using the phrase, "**We need to have a budget meeting**," we will first explore the lower sections of your vocal range as follows:

"We need to have a budget meeting. Can I go even lower? We need to have a budget meeting."

First, prepare your body: Stand tall. If you are seated, sit as if you are standing, spine straight, feet beneath your shoulders and not crossed, shoulders square, chest high, head perched on top. Warm-up your voice by making sounds like a foghorn. Do that a couple of times.

Good.

Now from way down in the basement of your vocal range, say, "We need to have a budget meeting."

Once more time, trying to go even lower.

Notice the tendency to lower your chin and dip your head down to reach the lower pitches.

You have just used an extreme form of **Chest Voice;** add a little volume and some emotion and you can imitate a lion.

At the opposite end of the pitch, the scale is falsetto. Falsetto is easily heard as the vocal quality is higher than most people speak. More easily discernable and enabled in the male voice, it is nevertheless functional in female voices as well.

For our purposes here, we are going to take it to extremes, so we sound almost like a squeak toy or Mickey Mouse.

"We need to have a budget meeting. It's such a beautiful day. Ouch! I stubbed my toe!"

How did you do? Please don't say you can't do it, because everyone, everyone can squeak like Mickey Mouse. If you smile it is much easier. Try it with a big happy smile on your face. Okay. Now just for fun, try it with a more serious expression.

This is not to say that you will ever use either the extreme low or high ends of your range for a presentation but knowing how large your range is, allows you to more freely explore what variety you have to offer.

Just below that silly squeak tone lies **Head Voice.**

To explore what it feels like, imagine you are trying to comfort a lost and frightened child. You are concerned about the child's well-being and can understand their need for gentle safety.

"It's okay. It's okay. Don't worry. We'll find Mommy and Daddy."

Go ahead and try it.

Notice that the voice is light, not very loud, and has warmth in it, a little like a songbird warbling away happily. Notice the expression on your face, and how it feels physically in your face, your jaw, your throat.

This time, repeat the same comforting words but say them as if frustrated, even a little angry.

What happened to the quality of the voice? To the physical feeling in your face? To the tension in your jaw and throat?

Go back and repeat the phrase for the first time: gentle, warm, comforting.

Now let's investigate **Mixed Voice**

Add a little volume to the Head Voice, as if the child was 3 arm lengths away. Add more as if the child is across the room. What happened to the quality of the voice? Were you able to keep the warmth and lightness or did it change?

Just like a parrot can mix and match sound quality to sound like a budgie one minute and a rough and ready old-time gunslinger the next, mixed voice is a combination of Head Voice and Chest Voice. The proportions of each can and will change depending on your intention and your own natural voice. Some individuals are more predisposed to Head Voice, others to Chest Voice, and will be more comfortable mixing more of their natural state into the blend.

The voices are not dependent on the pitch (how high or low the sound) although the head voice tends to be higher and chest voice lower. Rather, it is a vocal quality and it depends on which resonating chambers we are using; head voice uses the resonators in the sinuses, chest voice uses the resonators in the thoracic area.

When speakers are learning these concepts they often think that chest voice is the larger voice, lower, more commanding, more easily heard. Women are often told they must access their lower register to be taken seriously.

It's not completely true.

If we stay in the chest voice all the time, we limit expression, we harm our vocal cords, we sound artificial, and we lose the attention of our listeners, because, quick frankly, it is boring. Speakers that stay in chest voice are known as the modern miracle cure for insomnia. Furthermore, although it seems louder to us inside our heads, the sound does not travel well; it tends to die about an arm's length away from the speaker's mouth. If we add volume to chest voice, it will carry a little farther, but the quality of sound becomes harsh, strident, and not at all pleasant to listen to. The audience may feel like they are being scolded and therefore will be less receptive to the speaker's words.

On the other hand, speaking only in head voice isn't good either. The head voice carries far better than does chest voice, yes, but the pure head voice doesn't instill great trust in the speaker's competence and value. Delivered solely in head voice, the speaker's message may appear optional, even fluffy. The head voice sounds quieter to us because it doesn't spend much time bouncing around inside the sinus cavities before it leaves the body, but it carries much farther.

Consider the orchestra. The timpani is pounding, the double basses are supplying the bass lines, the trombones and trumpets are blaring, the strings are sawing away, and over it all, a single flute soaring up in the troposphere can be heard, its melody line crystal clear above the cacophony of sound below. That's the power of head voice.

A steady diet of only flute music is no better than nothing but double-bass lines. Unsupported head voice can be thin, unimpressive, and when the volume is added, strident, nasal, and even whiny. Provided not too much breath is used, the head voice does not harm the vocal mechanism in any way, but speakers using only head voice must use stronger body language and attitude to appear knowledgeable and confident.

A flute cannot take the place of a tuba, and a trumpet cannot replace a clarinet. Together though, they create music that reaches the hearts of the listeners. A speaker cannot use only head voice or chest voice, but rather must be able to take advantage of the head voice's agility, the chest voice's strength, the combined power and resonance of the mixed voice, and be able to transition between them seamlessly.

Gads! It could seem to be intimidating and beyond reach except ….
there are some tricks, some tools of the trade to make it all easier
to accomplish. Yea! We'll get to that as soon as we dispel some
myths about vocal projection.

VOCAL PROJECTION

Students of the dramatic arts and theatre must learn to say their
lines such that people in the back rows can hear them clearly. In the
theatre world, it's called projection. Novice students of the art
immediately think of V**olume**, and there is some of that in the
recipe to be sure. There's a heaping helping of R**esonance** in there,
too, controlled E**nergy** adds the flavor, and a giant dollop of **Support**
holds the cake together.

You may have heard that the secret to vocal project lies in the
diaphragm and that's completely true. The subject of never-ending
debate, however, concerns how we engage and control the
diaphragm. Not enough diaphragmatic support leaves the voice

weak, too much and the voice lacks nuance and expression (not to mention that it is exhausting!)

Tightening the diaphragm to the extreme is biologically counter-productive. Remember that to breathe deeply, low and slow, the diaphragm must flatten to make room for lung inhalation and return to its dome shape to push the unwanted air back out. If we have our diaphragm tightened up like a 2 by 4, we cannot breathe properly, and if we can't breathe properly, we get breathless. If we feel breathless, we can't think properly. We tense up, instigating the release of adrenalin which further reduces the amount of oxygen to our higher thinking functions, the result of which is that our worst fears are realized, and we forget what we went up to the podium to say and do. Yikes!

The solution I offer may seem more than a little odd, but it works brilliantly if you are willing to learn. I call it Making Diamonds and it involves your cheeks. Not the ones on your face.

MAKING DIAMONDS

What does it take to make a diamond?

It takes carbon, pressure and time.

What does it take to support vocal control yet not interfere with breathing?

It takes the engagement of the body's core.

What do the two of these have to do with each other?

When what we want is to make our diaphragm act like a trampoline, bouncy and resilient, and we want to make it automatic so we don't have to think about it, we need to make our very own diamonds.

EXERCISE

Stand in neutral, chest high, arms loose at your sides, shoulders square, feet directly underneath them.

Now tighten your diaphragm. Tighten it hard. Tighten it as if you are about to get hit in the abdomen with a sledgehammer. Hold it, hold it, hold it.

Release.

How did you feel? How are your shoulders? Your neck? Your throat? Could you do that for 60 or 90 minutes? Were you able to breathe properly? Did you even think about breathing? Not very relaxing, is it?

Wouldn't it be awful if that's what we had to do to make ourselves heard? Yet that's what concentrating on tightening your diaphragm for vocal support does.

Now, tighten your Gluteus Maximus. And Minimus. The back of your front, your derriere, your kiester, your bottom, your bum. Just your bum. Tighten it hard, but just the backside. You are adding the pressure needed to make a diamond.

Hold a moment longer and check your diaphragm. It should feel engaged but pliable. Check your posture. You are likely standing tall and proud. Check your core. Is your lower abdomen engaged? Can you still belly breathe?

By engaging the gluteus muscles, you have engaged your core, and given energy to the diaphragm to do what it must to not only keep you alive but keep you being heard. It supports your voice allowing full resonance, projection, and agility without you even thinking about it. Engaging the core bolsters confidence, and encourages good breathing, thus removing the release of adrenalin and giving you a feeling of compact control over yourself. Go ahead and store all your nervous energy back there where it will not interfere with delivering your presentation masterfully.

The best part is that you will only need to concentrate your efforts back there a couple of times because the rewards are so great that it will become instant and automatic. You won't even know you're doing it! It does take a little preliminary effort to become accustomed to the feeling of an engaged core, but because it gives us such a powerful sense of assurance, it is well worth the effort.

ENUNCIATION

There is another completely vital component of vocal production, that being **Enunciation**.

Simply put, enunciation is how well we pronounce our words.

To pronounce words so they can be understood at a distance (whether using a microphone or not), requires energy in the mouth, specifically the lips and the tongue.

Many of us have Lazy Mouth. Our societies are becoming increasingly casual and so too is our use of language. Lazy pronunciations like gunna, woulda, shoulda, gimme, cuz, and so on are so common that most people scarcely think much about it, but excellent public speakers are not most people. If we want others to understand us, especially at a distance, our carefully chosen words must be given due respect and pronounced clearly and completely.

A body in motion tends to stay in motion. A body at rest tends to stay at rest. Sometimes it takes a little kick start to get us moving in the morning, but once we're out of bed and out the door, we can usually go all day.

To wake up our mouths from their usual state of doing only the bare minimum to make ourselves understood, try these exercises.

EXERCISE

This has the potential to be a little messy so you may want to watch out for that.

Stick your tongue out of your almost closed mouth just a little bit. Now blow so that the tongue flaps about in the breeze. This is called a Raspberry and there are few children in the world that have not perfected it. Do it with Attitude! It is excellent for loosening up that great big and strong tongue muscle. Repeat 3 or 4 times.

Next step: close your mouth so your lips are lighting touching. Now blow so that the lips flap about a bit. This is called a Motorboat, and it works very well for removing tension from the lips.

Step 3, and this is the potential messy part: Alternate the Raspberry and the Motorboat 3 or 4 times. Not only does it loosen up the mouth, but because it's also ridiculously silly it's a bit of fun and fun releases endorphins. Life just doesn't get any better... or does it?

EXERCISE

We carry enormous amounts of tension in our mouths, most especially in the tongue. It is strenuous enough to carry off a brilliant presentation without additional tension. This exercise is a bit rude to do in front of company, but it works like a hot diggedy!

Open your mouth wide. Now stick your tongue straight out of your head as far as you can. Not up, not down, not to one side, but straight out. Your lips should not touch the tongue. Use a mirror if you want to. Hold that stretch for a count of 5 and relax. You should feel it way down at the base of your tongue, down in the throat. Repeat a couple of times. I haven't found anything that works better for releasing tongue tension.

EXERCISE

Tongue Twisters require concentration and energy. The trick is to avoid adding tension in the mouth as that just makes the tongue twisters more difficult.

Try these:

Rubber baby buggy bumpers

Say it 5 times as quickly as you can. Hint: keep the lips and cheeks ultra-loose; it's more beneficial and more fun.

Red leather, yellow leather

5 times fast. This one is difficult if you have jaw tension. Wiggle your bottom jaw around a few times to loosen it up.

The sixth sick sheik's sixth sheep's sick.

This one is difficult. Try visualizing six sheiks who are not feeling well, each surrounded by six sheep, and with the 6th sheik's last sheep being sick. It might help.

Pheasant Plucker

Don't even try this if swearing is unacceptable to you.

I'm not the pheasant plucker.
I'm the pheasant plucker's son,
And I'm only plucking pheasants
'til the pheasant plucking's done.

Say it as quickly as possible, taking notice of the possible pitfalls.

As you can now see quite clearly, lack of respect for energized enunciation can profoundly change the meaning of your message!

While we must always speak the same language the audience understands, the speaking platform is not the place to show off your "street cred." The respect we demonstrate to language is the same respect you will receive for your speaking expertise.

CONSONANTS

N P J H G W K
M T D V Q X H
L Z S F C B R

The thing about consonants: there should be some.

When we are sitting in casual company, fairly close to the people with whom we are speaking, the value of clear consonants is important but not vital. We all read lips, whether we mean to or not, and so when words are not pronounced as clearly as they could be, we can still get the gist of the conversation by watching the face and the body for additional clues.

When we are addressing a group, however, or even when the person we are speaking to is farther away, the value of crisp and distinct consonants becomes more important.

The beginnings of words are usually clear enough; it is the word endings that are sacrificed because of lazy mouth or speed. Be honest with yourself; how clear is your pronunciation of the "t" at the end of "wouldn't?" Is it crisp or is it more dentalized and assumed? Try saying this phrase:

"I wouldn't go if I didn't have to."

Be honest. Was the "t" at the end of "wouldn't" or "didn't" crisp and slightly explosive or were they more imploded just inside your mouth?

From the speaker's spot, these kinds of pronunciation issues become magnified. Since only 7% of our message is received via the words we use, doesn't that make the pronunciation of your words critically important?

The letter "d" at the end of words is even more difficult than the "t." Since "d" requires even less energy than does "t" it is very often assumed rather than actually heard. Don't even get me started about the "g" at the end of running, jumping, eating and so on!

The gist of the message about consonants is to pay more attention to them from the platform than from across the table in your kitchen. It will make you seem more accomplished, and more professional. Just don't overdo it; the last thing you want to be seen as is pompous or arrogant!

VOWELS

Vowel pronunciation is dependent on an accent. Everyone has an accent that can vary not only from country to country but district to district and social class to social class. Consider Canada or the United States: Eastern Canadians speak very differently than those from the West Coast, and those from the southern United States pronounce things very different than those from Boston.

Vowels are generally described as tall (think British nobility) or as wide (think Texas). There is no correct one way to pronounce vowels unless you are an actor or are singing classical music. Still, there are a few things to keep in mind.

1. Many vowels are actually a combination of sounds creating **diphthongs**. Consider the long A as in hay, say, weigh, brave. We begin the sound as one would expect, but we finish with a long E.
    Give it a try and see how incomplete the pronunciation feels without the final E.

2. The long I, as in eye, mine, bike, is a combination of ah and ee.
3. The O, as in over, open, core, is not completed until we add a long U as in, you.
4. Vowel combinations. Oy veh! The combination of, ough, can be pronounced 10 different ways, even without taking accents into account.

The important thing to remember is to pay attention to your pronunciation. An audience will accept almost anything as long as it is consistent and clear enough for them to understand that's just the way you do it.

CARE OF THE VOICE

Just as we take care of our eyes, our skin, even our fingernails, our voice benefits from just a little bit of nurturing. The environment of the vocal mechanism is much like a rain forest: moist, warm, and delicate. We want the vocal mechanism to always be agile, loose, and relaxed. Anything that creates tension or tightness is to be avoided. Think of your vocal folds as spaghetti cooked al dente i.e. slightly soft and pliable. Tension and abuse of the folds turn them into raw spaghetti, and you know how easily those long, thin strands of pasta break.

If you've ever experienced chapped lips, you know how irritating and sometimes downright painful it can be. You also know how difficult it is to heal them. The chapping is caused by cold air chafing and irritating the moist and tender tissues of the lips. Now think about yelling. When we yell, we tense our vocal folds and force tremendous amounts of air over the delicate tissues, in effect "chapping" our vocal folds. This is typical of laryngitis. If we continue abusing the voice this way, the inflamed areas begin to form a bit of scar tissue, that can eventually form vocal nodes. Individuals with vocal nodes have voices that sound raspy and raw and thin. The only treatment for vocal nodes is surgery, and it is not always successful.

Imagine sitting at the beach, relaxed and pleasantly warm. Suddenly someone throws a pail of cold water on you. Even if you were expecting it, chances are that your muscles will tighten, your attitude will do a major shift, and it will take a while to return to your previous state of rest. The same is true of the voice. Ice cold beverages before you are going to give a presentation will not do your voice any favors.

We wouldn't dream of pouring acid on a grand piano, yet so many speakers believe that lemon water is a refreshing and cleansing drink. Coffee contains a substantial amount of acid as do spicy foods.

Whispering is a huge no-no. Whispering forces the vocal folds NOT to vibrate as air passes over them. That creates tension (already a bad idea), and because we still want to be heard we send large amounts of fast-moving air over the already brittle cords. What happens? Chapping. Inflammation, and pain.

Here's a list of the dos and don'ts for taking care of the professional speaking voice.

Care of the Voice

- ✓ No forcing to avoid nodes
- ✓ No smoking
- ✓ Minimize caffeine and other acids like lemon
- ✓ Minimize ice water and never drink it before a speech
- ✓ Minimize coughing – try drinking water instead
- ✓ Rest

If SICK (and especially if you have to speak

- ✓ Rest at least 12-24 hours (no talking)
- ✓ No whispering
- ✓ No ice water
- ✓ No caffeine
- ✓ No menthol cough drops
- ✓ No antihistamines
- ✓ No nasal sprays
- ✓ Yes to gentle herb teas
- ✓ Yes to salt water (not too salty)
- ✓ Absolute yes to chicken broth (again not too salty)
- ✓ Yes to room temperature water and lots of it

A speaker with a healthy, agile, and resonant voice will always be more effective than one without. Our personality, our professionalism, and our value to the listeners is built into the way we speak, a task made much more difficult when our voices are depleted. Take care of it well.

Rosemarie Barnes

CONFIDENT STAGES

Chapter 9

Confident Physical Delivery Skills

CONFIDENT PHYSICAL DELIVERY SKILLS

As individuals who speak to others either one to one, one to a few, or one to many, we understand and appreciate the extraordinary power of words. Words and language have power far greater than physical force so we may be forgiven for thinking that the most important part of a presentation lies in our choice of words.

I'm sorry to have to tell you, but it just isn't so.

In fact, according to the FBI, Quantico, and Dr. Mehrabian (who did in-depth research on this topic as it relates to negotiation skills), only 7% of the message we send is received via the words we use. Only 7%! The full breakdown of how messages are received looks like this:

7%   Words (verbal)

38%   Voice (para-verbal)

55%   Physical (non-verbal)

If only 7% of our message is transmitted via words, the implications are that they had better be really good words and that we had best pay some pretty strong attention to the other 93%. The 38% received via vocal tonality and finesse is covered in the Confident Vocal Delivery Skills unit but right here and right now let's unpack the power of Physical Delivery Skills.

The most wonderful thing about these skills is that not only do they assist the speaker in engaging the listeners, they also help the speaker remember the presentation itself. Muscle memory is strong and has a remarkably long shelf life. Consider riding a bicycle: once you have learned how, your body remembers. It may be years, even decades since you last hopped onto your bike, but give yourself 2 or 3 minutes. Your body will very quickly resurrect that knowledge from stored muscle memory and off you go. This is the power of kinesiology; we don't need to run "how to pedal" through the memory banks of the brain for our muscles to respond. For presentations, choreographing a step forward to accompany a statement and then reinforcing that muscle memory via rehearsal, means that when we take that seemingly innocent step forward at the appropriate time, that simple movement will remind us of what we were going to say, and again, off we go.

I have never, nor will I ever advocate memorizing a presentation for so many reasons, the most important being that a memory lapse is the single greatest contributor to speakers' fear. Using muscle memory, however, acts like a cue card or a neon light shining directly on the next topic in the presentation. It works brilliantly as a mental memory jog for the speaker.

For the listener, the speaker's physical delivery skills can greatly enhance or completely eviscerate the speaker's message.

EXERCISE

Try this little exercise: Say, "Yes, yes, yes," while indicating, "No," with your head. It can be a little disconcerting! Add a gesture that matches the voice. Do it again but this time with a gesture that matches the head.

Now try it the opposite way by saying, "No, no, no," but indicating the opposite with your head. Now add the gesture first matching the voice, then one last time with the gesture matching the head.

Once again, it feels very strange, and yet we do it more often than we think! Now consider the message the listeners receive: yes and no at the same time!

Here's the real kicker: for all our attention to words and language, when there is a conflict between what we see and what we hear, the message sent by the body is perceived to be the truth. Learning to control what your body is doing while your mouth and brain and happily chatting away is arguably the most important skill a presenter can acquire.

BODY LANGUAGE

Body Language is a large and well-researched topic. It is complicated and can seem a little overwhelming. As a speaker, you have so many things to remember and it may seem that since you have been successfully communicating since you were born, spending time considering whether your body is helping or hurting your case to be of little importance. That is, until you understand that over half your message is being received by what your arms, legs, torso, and face are up to!

Let's start with **Energy**.

Your energy level affects how your message is projected and received. In the simplest terms,

High energy = good

Low energy= not as good

Taken to extremes though, excessive energy is hard to control and can distract from your content. We've all seen presenters resembling the Eveready Battery Bunny clanging their figurative cymbals without end; by the time they've completed the session, we're exhausted and have learned nothing. Too much, too fast, too emphatic and usually combined with too much information can leave us feeling like we've just been through a tsunami and in need of rest! Extreme low energy or casualness can leave an audience unimpressed even if the information is of vital importance.

When in doubt, show your listeners the kind of energy you would like them to absorb and mirror back to you.

Posture

Perfect posture varies as the presentation goes on, of course, but always begins from neutral, i.e. straight spine in all directions, feet under shoulders, knees loose, torso square on hips, chest high, arms at sides, and head perched on top like the treasure it is.

Straight Spine

A straight spine sends the message that you are a straight shooter, confident, and composed. Unlike our little wooden figure (let's give it a non-gender specific name like say, Billie) a straight spine does not mean you have a metal rod up your back, unable to move. A straight spine allows you to breathe properly, move easily, and provide assurance of excellence to both speaker and listener. Incorrect spine alignment can make the presenter appear untrustworthy, and even careless.

Feet Under Shoulders

When asked to put their feet directly under the shoulders, many people take a stance that is far too wide and resembling a Sumo Wrestler. Here's how to accurately determine the perfect shoulder-width apart stance:

1. Stand with feet together, heels and bunions touching.
2. Assume the Mary Poppins or ballet first position, by keeping both heels touching but spreading the fronts (bunions) apart thus forming a V with the feet.

3. Keeping the balls of your feet on firm ground, rotate your heels so they are directly behind the toes.
4. Voila! Your feet are directly under your shoulders just like Billie.

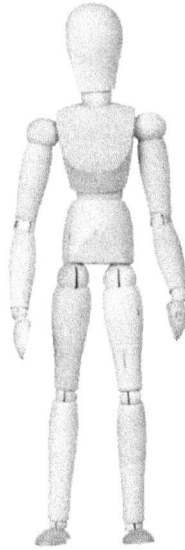

With your feet in this position, you will feel grounded and can move in any direction easily. Crossing your legs, your feet, or your arms broadcasts insecurity, fear, and a need for support; avoid at all costs.

Loose Knees

Loose knees do not mean spaghetti legs, but rather, simply keeping them unlocked. Locking up any joint when you present is just asking for pain later. Keep your goose loose.

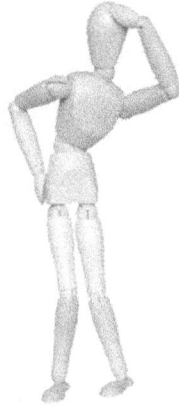

Tilted Torso

Tilting from the waist or hips wither forward/backward or side to side can quite literally make a presenter look crooked; it does no favors to anyone. Stand tall and proud.

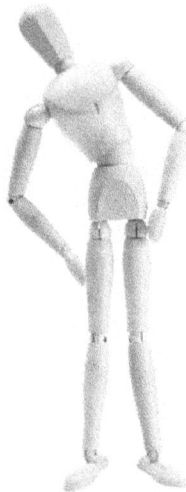

Leaning

Similar to tilting, leaning on anything can send the message that your opinion cannot stand on its own. This includes putting weight on one leg more than the other or physically leaning on a table or lectern. Believing they are sending a message of casual friendliness or even as a show of confidence, it can have the opposite effect of appearing arrogant or uncaring.

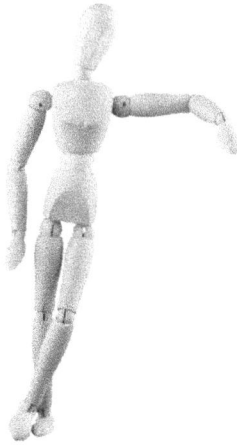

Chest High

Keeping the chest high does a couple of things: firstly, it allows the presenter to breathe properly thereby keeping their brains well-oxygenated, and secondly, it sends a message of confidence and pride (not the arrogant kind). A sunken chest portrays the opposite indicating self-centered and inward-focused attention and even lack of focus.

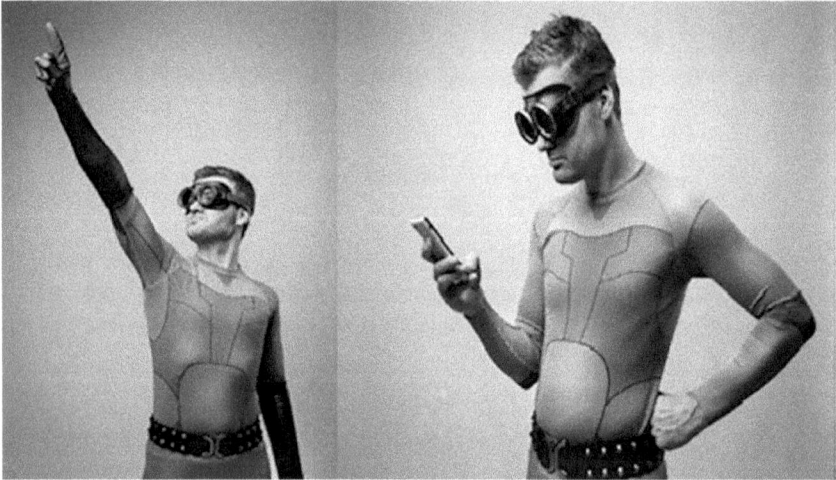

An additional benefit of keeping the chest high is that it forces the shoulders to be square thus causing the arms to simply hang naturally at the sides.

GESTURES

On the periphery of posture lives the world of **Gestures.**

Gestures and their appropriateness are dictated by multiple factors, among them:

Size of room and size of the audience
Desired impact on the audience
Personality of the presenter.

Generally, for live presentations, the larger the room, the larger the gestures must be to enhance the meaning of the words. Recorded video, however, demand that gestures fit into the size of the frame and so remain well contained.

Since we do most (but not all) of our gesturing with our arms, let's begin there. In casual conversation our arms and hands know what to do; just try telling someone how big that fish was without using gestures! For presenters, deliberate and thoughtful gestures enhance our message; careless and casual gestures can just as easily dilute it.

Arm movements do more than enhance our message; they also show the listeners a bit of our personality. Calmer presenters tend to use slower gestures than either frightened or excited presenters. Expansive personalities find expansive gestures to be comfortable while more introverted types like to keep their gestures smaller. Home base for the arms is to allow them to simply drop down from the squared shoulders straight down the sides of the torso. This is neutral. This is where we begin and end.

Avoid:

Hands in pockets: Even though we may be trying to look casual and relaxed, hands in pockets is received as arrogant and even worse, that we are hiding something. Don't do it. Ever.

Gripping the lectern: Message received is that we need support.

Touching the lectern microphone: Sends a message that we are fidgety, unsure, and with little confidence.

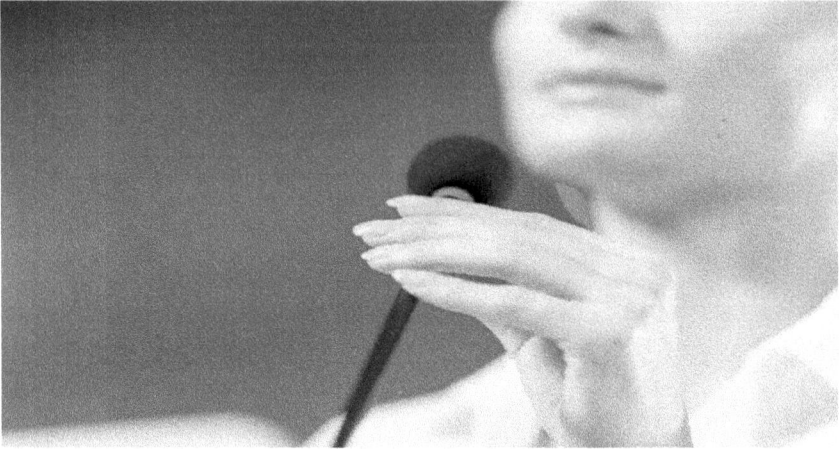

Touching any part of our body: holding our own hands, steepled fingers, hands-on-hips, crossed arms, crossed legs, crossed feet, all send a message of insecurity. We may feel justified in using our hands in these ways as it feels good to us, but remember that our comfort is not the most important factor; **everything we do as presenters is to send the message we wish our listeners to receive.**

Velcro Elbows: In line with touching any part of our body, gesturing a la Tyrannosaurus Rex with tiny little arms is a safety move, designed to make the presenter feel better; if you are going to make a gesture, do it fully to instill confidence in your listeners that you are secure in your message.

FINGERS

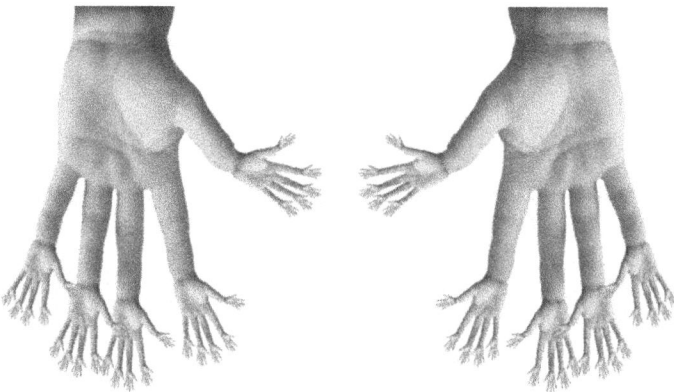

Gesturing with your fingers can get us into so much trouble! When you are giving a presentation, leave your fingers at home! Pointing at another individual can easily be construed as accusatory. The reason flight attendants use two fingers or even their entire hand to indicate the exits in an airplane cabin is so that no one can feel they are being singled out. Even when taking questions, an open palm at the end of an extended arm is welcoming while pointing a finger is far less so.

Finger symbols like a V for victory or peace, or the very common thumbs up for A-OK have very different meanings in different cultures.

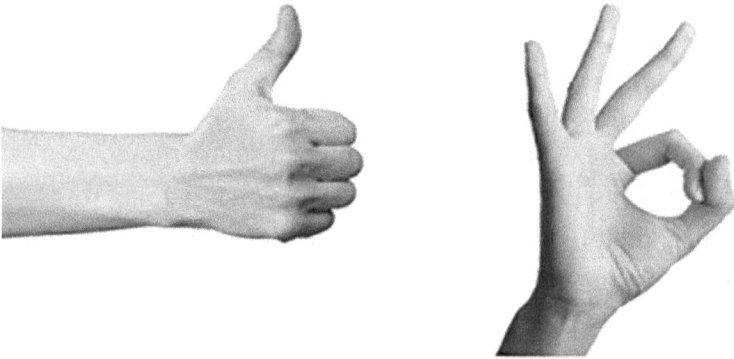

In many parts of the world, for example, the thumbs-up sign has the same meaning as does the middle finger salute in Canada and the US. Similarly, the circular An OK sign can also signify something very rude.

Avoid finger gestures at all costs! The possibility of negative reactions is not worth the risk.

MOVEMENT

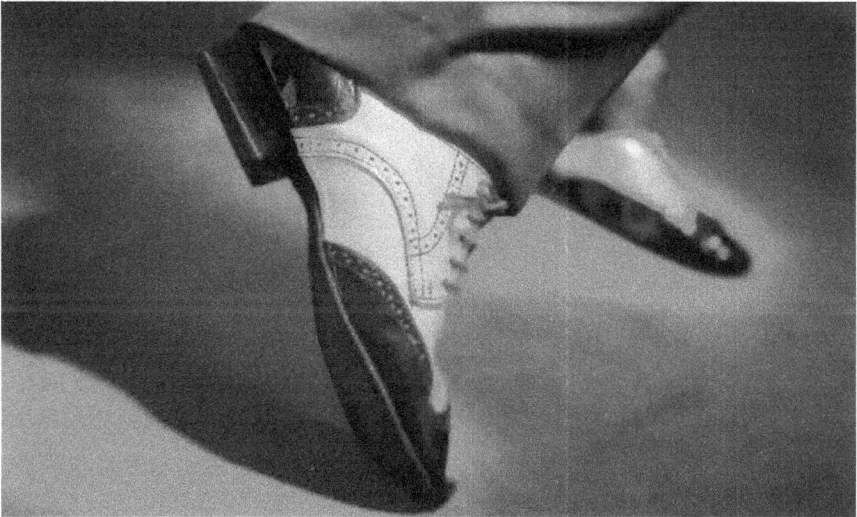

There seems to be a common thought among presenters that wandering from side to side in the presentation space is acceptable and appropriate because so many do it. Perhaps the belief is that the more space they take up, the more important they appear. Perhaps these presenters think they are connecting better with their listeners. Perhaps the idea is to look relaxed and comfortable.

WRONG WRONG WRONG!

Let's dissect this a little bit.

Remember Dr. Mehrabian and the formula for the way we receive messages?

7%   Words

38% Voice

55% Physical

55% of the way we receive messages is through physical means: standing, sitting, moving. If we spend that 55% pacing across the space, what message are the listeners receiving? How is that movement contributing to our message? Remember that it is the powerful 7%, the words, that are either enhanced or diluted by the remaining 93% (the vocal and physical messages) so why, oh why, would we waste the opportunity by paying insufficient attention to the way we move? Why would we risk losing listener attention to our precious 7%, our words, by distracting the listeners through idle movement? To move or not to move, that is the question, and there is a solid answer and a new rule:

NEW RULE

If you have nowhere to go and no reason to get there,

STAY STILL

I am not suggesting that we must stand like a robot with our feet nailed to the floor; quite the contrary, movement has great power to enhance our meaning. What I am saying is that when 55% of our message comes from physical means, then we must pay that facet much more attention than most people normally do.

But then, since you are actively striving to improve your presentation skills, you are not most people!

Dispelling the Movement Myth

As covered in the Use of Space unit, (but well worth repeating) there are some excellent reasons for movement and a well-believed myth that needs to be dispelled. The myth is that moving from side to side in the space helps presenters connect with their listeners.

Consider what happens to the listeners on one side of the audience while the speaker is close to them: they feel important, special. What happens when the presenter wanders off to the other side? No more important or special and in fact, even a little bit like yesterday's leftovers. Speaker and listener are now disengaged. What do we do when we disengage? Our minds wander like the speaker is doing. Outcomes the phone to check messages. We check out emotionally, too, and when the speaker returns to our side of the audience, they must re-engage with us. Boing Boing Boing! Some presenters do this so continually we could be excused for thinking they are trying to get in their 10,000 steps a day while addressing their audience!

And what do we think of the speaker that boomerangs around and expects us to keep pace? Not good!

Purposeful movement can and does add credence and emphasis to our words, but does not help us, "fill the space." The best way to do that is with our Presence, not our feet!

Purposeful movement can and does activate the presenter's muscle memory, one of the most powerful memory joggers we have.

Purposeful movement enhances our message.

Idle movement does not.

Full Stop.

FACIAL EXPRESSION

Our facial expressions are an enormously important part of every presentation. Some people's faces are more expressive than others and that's okay. Some of us broadcast our every thought across our faces while others are quite difficult to read. There is no good or bad here, only awareness.

Let's start with the eyes, the proverbial windows to our soul.

One of the most important things a presenter must do is to make direct eye contact with as many participants as possible. And not just once, but often. Why? Because it builds trust better than anything else can.

EXERCISE

This exercise will help you internalize the power of eye contact. You will need a partner so ask a significant other, a teenager, a sibling, or even a willing stranger at a bus stop. Using the phrase,

"We need to have a budget meeting," take turns delivering the line first looking at the ceiling, the floor, over their heads, as if someone else just walked into the area, and finally, directly at them. Notice how the strength of the message changes. A presenter's job is to make the point personal and powerful. Which one worked the best for you?

Everyone wants to be seen, to feel special, to feel that the presenter is speaking directly to them, and the easiest and absolutely most powerful way to accomplish that is to make recurrent connections with them via eye contact. Hold the contact only up to about 3 seconds: more and it feels like staring, less and it is only a fleeting glance and holds no meaning. Make an effort to connect with every single person in attendance; if that's impossible, do the best you can.

Next on the list is the smile. Smiling makes us approachable by giving the impression of friendliness. Horrible news shared with even an empathetic smile is easier to hear. Good news shared with a beaming smile makes the news even better. Smiling raises the cheekbones and increases the size of the resonating cavities making our voices more energized and pleasant to hear. The eyes close a little and the outside edges crinkle, the eyebrows are drawn down a wee bit and there is full facial involvement.

Where the sincere smile is warm and causes us to mirror a smile in return, the fake smile is disturbing. The fraudulent smile can very quickly destroy connection and trust and utterly ruin the opportunity to improve the lives of the listeners or get a signature on the deal.

Compare these two images and examine your responses to them.

Who do you believe? Who seems more open? Who is more welcoming? To whom do you want to listen?

There is such a thing as smiling too much and depending on the topic, inappropriate smiling can create an atmosphere of superficiality and minimize the importance of the topic. As a rule, though, as long as you believe what you are saying, and truly care about the impact of your topic on the listeners, your face, your eyes, and your smile will be sincere, believable, and trustworthy.

SUMMARY

Over half our presentation is shared via physiological means so it warrants paying attention to what our bodies are saying. Our verbal message is our stock and trade but by enhancing that message by aligning the verbal and the non-verbal, we create far, far more impact. If the two messages are not aligned, it is always the physical one that is taken as true. The energy level we use to present our topic must be high, but not so high as to exhaust both the presenter and the listener. Good posture sends a message of confidence and allows the speaker to breathe properly and the brain to function fully. Gestures must be meaningful and full-bodied so they will be received as honest and assured, and avoidance of using finger gestures will help us stay clear of interpretation trouble. Move with purpose, make eye contact, and smile sincerely and honestly. Remember that everything we do physically will enhance or detract from our words, so paying close attention to what we are doing while we are speaking is well worth the time and effort.

CONFIDENT STAGES

Chapter 10

Confident Use of Space

CONFIDENT USE OF SPACE

In order to be heard and understood, we must be seen. Even if we don't think we do, everyone reads lips. We also read faces, and body language, and a myriad of other things. It is so interesting to know that if our listeners can't see us well, they will often complain that they couldn't hear us well. The reverse is true as well; if they can't hear us well, they will squirm about trying to get a better view.

It is the speaker's responsibility to ensure we can be seen and while that might sound simple, often it is somewhat more complicated than we might guess. Some areas in our presentation spaces are naturally more powerful than others, and as excellent presenters, we can use that to our advantage.

Let's begin with terminology and for this where we are going to speak in theatre terms. Please don't be alarmed. Speakers do not require theatre training! We simply need shared terminology for understanding, and theatre nomenclature is thorough and convenient.

To begin, we are going to call our presentation space the **stage.** It doesn't matter whether we are presenting in a boardroom, a lecture hall, a ballroom, or a restaurant, whatever space we must work in is referred to as the **stage.**

```
 _____
|              UPSTAGE               |
|                                    |
STAGE RIGHT              STAGE LEFT
|                                    |
|              DOWNSTAGE             |
 _____
```

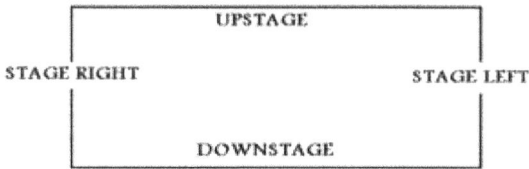

AUDIENCE / MIRROR

The first thing you need to know is that stage descriptions and stage directions are always given from the presenter's point of view, not from that of the listener. Stage right then is the presenter's right. Stage left is the presenter's left. It makes good sense that way, because the audience doesn't care which is stage left or stage right; the presenter does.

The part of the space furthest away from the audience is called Upstage, the part closest to them is Downstage. There is some history to this. Years ago, when travelling bards and minstrels spread the news and provided some small amount of entertainment, they took their belongings with them using horse/donkey/oxen pulled wagons and carts. When it was time to perform, they would, of course, release their cart from the beast of burden power source causing the front end to become lower than the back. It worked very well because now the musicians at the higher end could still be seen and heard; the back end of the "stage" was quite literally, "Up," while the front was lower, or "down." That description of Upstage and Downstage has stuck throughout time. Downstage is the edge closest to the audience, Upstage is farthest away, Stage Right and Stage Left as seen from the performer's point of view.

Every stage can be divided into sections, the uses of which will become clear momentarily.

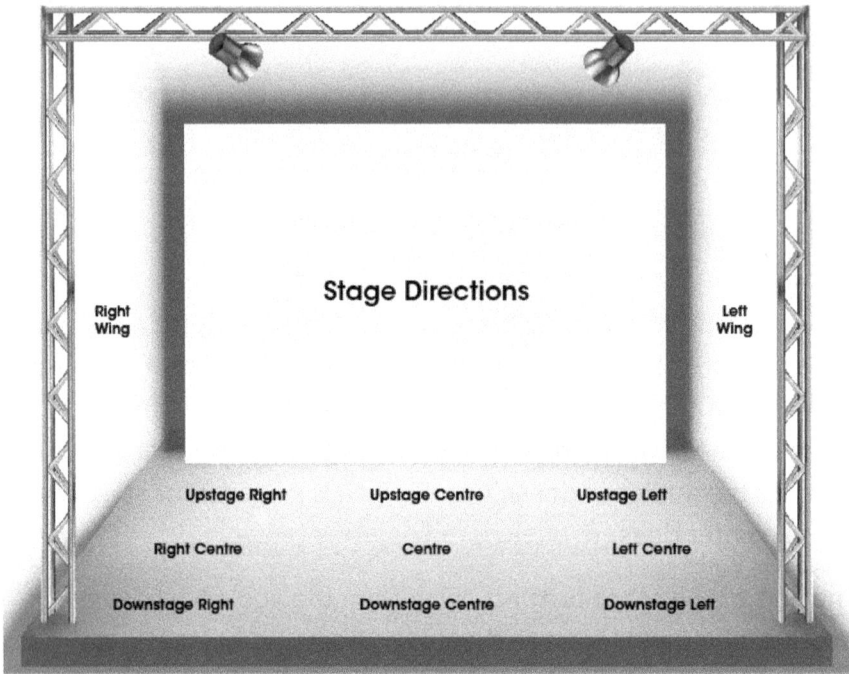

Stage Directions

Right Wing

Left Wing

Upstage Right   Upstage Centre   Upstage Left

Right Centre   Centre   Left Centre

Downstage Right   Downstage Centre   Downstage Left

AUDIENCE

We can see that the stage left is the audience's right. Stage right is the audience's left, and that's okay because the audience doesn't care what the sections of the stage are called. We do.

The question that may be at the tip of your tongue is, "Why do we care? What do we need to know that for?"

Knowing the parts of the stage and what they are called is only for clarity and ease of conversation just as an auto mechanic's work is so much simpler when he/she talks about a manifold or a piston instead of calling it, "that thingy over there." Using correct nomenclature is also very helpful when speaking to event planners, or audio/visual and lighting technicians and makes us sound terribly clever.

Regardless of your presentation space, (your stage) each section of the stage has some advantages and disadvantages so let's break them down.

Stage Right: In the western world at least, reading and writing start at the top left of the page. We learn this as babies when Mommy or Daddy read us stories and show us pictures beginning from the upper left. We learn this so well and so quickly that it would be absurd to think of beginning anywhere else: things begin on the left. The audience's left. Stage Right for us. If we have a choice, it is always best to enter the space from Stage Right because it is comfortable for the listeners and opens the door to the Like, Know, Trust, and Respect relationship to begin.

However, if you are trying to be, "edgy," or if you are going to recount events starting from the endpoint, entering from Stage Left can be very effective. If space considerations will not allow you to enter from Stage Right or Left, then enter where you can; you will just have to wear a bigger smile and spread some of your sparkling charisma just a little farther so your listeners will feel that all is right with the world.

Stage Left: Just as reading begins on the left, it ends on the right, so if you wish to leave your audience feeling fully satisfied and not even notice which direction you took off to, then exit Stage Left. This area is where you want to conclude a story or example.

Centre Stage: This is the standard power place. Centre Stage is where you want to be when you are making your strong points or stating your point of view.

Downstage: Stronger than Upstage simply because you are closer to your listeners.

Upstage: Great area to use if you are delivering negative opinions or bad news. The distance, even if it is only a foot or two acts as a buffer and makes the announcement easier to hear.

Front of House: the reception area, where tickets are purchased, the main doors into the venue.

Backstage: space in the wings (sides of the stage) and the area behind the stage, both shielded from audience view

Movement: Movement from Upstage to Downstage strengthens the message. The risk is that moving too quickly can intimidate the listeners. Moving downstage can invite connection and more intimacy. The opposite movement, from Downstage to Upstage will weaken the impact of your words (even if you don't want it to); increasing the space between you and your listeners can serve as a buffer for both. Lateral movement has also been covered in the Confident Physical Delivery Skills unit, but for now, let me say this loudly and clearly:

If you don't have anywhere to go and no particular reason to get there, for goodness sake, stop wearing out your shoes pacing like a caged animal in a zoo! It does not help you connect with your listeners and it can make you look like you are suffering from some sort of neurosis.

Lateral Movement

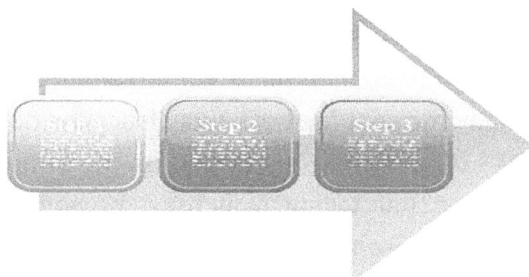

Lateral movement is excellent for creating a visual for chronological events or directions. Use Stage Right for the oldest of the events or step 1, move closer to Centre Stage for the next in line, then on to Stage Left to complete the sequence. Politicians and Talk Show Hosts like to designate areas for certain topics. Aficionados of late-night talk shows know that when the host steps into one particular spot on the set, it is time for the monologue; when they move over to the desk it is time for a guest to appear. Politicians routinely give good news from one side, bad news from the other, until we are lulled into satisfied expectations. Then, when he/she says something negative from the good news spot, we filter it through the good news expectation and respond less negatively than we normally would.

All this information is well and good if you are presenting somewhere that allows you the option of movement, but what if you are in a crowded boardroom or even speaking to a client over coffee? There are still some things we can do to make the best of any space in which we find ourselves.

Zone of Strength

In every room, there is a power spot, a place where all eyes focus and from where the individual standing can most easily assume power and control. It is the first place we see when we look in a room and is usually the seat farthest away from the door. You will never see a CEO's office where the desk is on the same wall as the door, or with his/her chair facing away from the point of entry. The same is true of meeting rooms where most commonly, the leader of the meeting faces the door and has a clear sight of each individual in attendance complete with their comings and goings.

Height

If you are looking for control, higher is better. If you are looking for comfortable and intimate, lower is better. If you are looking for engagement, use both. There is a reason why individuals trying to take a stand, "draw themselves up to their full height," and why we sit down to have a confidential or more intimate conversation. One of the most obvious reasons for a raised platform is so that the audience can see you. It is even more important that you can see them; you cannot connect with them if you can't make some sort of contact with them. In a formal presentation space, that's already taken care of by means of a stage or podium. (Yes, a podium is what we stand on. It's a lectern that many speakers stand behind.) If you are in a meeting without a podium to make you taller, for goodness sake, at least **stand-up!** Not only stand up but stand up proud. The space is yours for whatever amount of time you have, so make it yours by taking control of it. Own it. Fill it. If you are small of stature, not to worry. Fill the space with your energy and confidence and you will be the tallest and most commanding person in the room.

Sometimes in a lecture hall or presentation theatre, the speaker is actually lower than the audience who is watching and listening from tiered seating. While this may seem to be a disadvantage from the height perspective, these seating arrangement forces focus to the presenter, and as long as he/she fills the space with positive and directed energy, they will still be perceived to be in the power spot.

SEATING ARRANGEMENTS

Sometimes we have no control over the seating arrangement, so we use other tools to engage our listeners. If we are fortunate enough to dictate the arrangement of audience chairs, there are many options depending on our intention, the kind of interactions we are going to instigate, the results we wish to create, and of course, the physical comfort and safety of the audience. These 7 possibilities are the most common:

Option 1: Theatre Style

This option is seating only, arranged in rows, focused on the area farthest away from the main doors. Some presenters shy away from a center aisle (especially when they are speaking to sell) because shorter rows with an aisle between them make it easier for people to leave. When only the ends of long rows are available for egress, someone leaving will bring attention to themselves, and most people will elect to just stay. Long, straight rows are reminiscent of the discipline of schools and call on participants to be on best behavior. Many presenters use this seating arrangement because it is the simplest means of audience and room control.

There are some negatives attached to this arrangement as well, the first being safety. In an emergency, the lack of a center aisle makes it more difficult to evacuate the audience which can cause panic.

The other less obvious result of this arrangement is that wide rows make it more difficult for the presenter to engage the individuals at each end, and more often than not they respond by pacing across the stage like the aforementioned caged animal patrolling his territory. A long, narrower audience arrangement removes the need for making special connections with the individuals on the ends, but now, the people in the back may feel excluded. To counter this little problem, some presenters leave the stage to meander down the aisles and to connect with the listeners seated closer to the doors. This strolling along may well make the presenter more visible to those seats, but it leaves those closer to the stage with nothing to look at and feeling a bit like yesterday's breakfast. It gives them a chance to check their watch, check their phone, or just check out.

Turning your back on your listeners is **NEVER** a good idea.

Option 2: Curved Theatre Style

In this arrangement, chairs are still in rows, but the ends of those rows curve around the stage in a slight horseshoe shape. The rows are still long and wide, but those on the periphery can still look directly at the stage without turning their heads. Formal enough to still inspire, the, "best behavior" mindset, it is more inviting than Option #1 and allows for better engagement between presenter and listener. This arrangement brings more of the audience closer to the presenter while still maintaining safety standards. The choice of a center aisle still exists or for large groups, 2 aisles separating a center section from side sections. More options to leave quietly are available, so presenters will have to rely on other tools to keep the audience in their seats.

Option 3: Straight Rows, classroom style

This option is identical to the first, Theatre Style, but with accompanying writing surfaces (tables or desks). Listeners can take notes easily which is very important for kinetic learning. Now they also have a place for their beverages, their pens, and so on and depending on the makeup of the group, that can be beneficial or detrimental to the presenter. Anytime it is comfortable for the listeners to have a cup of coffee or such, it is an opportunity for .... Noise and Garbage. Think about the sugar packets, the cream containers, the stir sticks. And what happens next? The granola bars, the candy wrappers, and to quote Dr. Seuss' Grinch, "oh, the noise, noise, noise, noise!"

Additionally, when people are sharing a table, they are sharing "common ground," which can inspire the urge to lean over and make comments with an elbow neighbor. While presenters work very hard to engage their listeners, what we do not always want is the audience to engage with each other while we are up there, doing our thing. That said, this style of seating is very good for having participants discuss a topic when we instruct them to do so.

Option 4: Dining Room style

This style is commonly used when the presentation is accompanied by a meal. Eight or 10 people are seated at round tables to share a meal, good conversation, and to be informed, inspired, or invited to participate in some way. When the time comes for the presenter to take to the stage, it requires that half of the room shuffle about for a bit in order to turn their chair around to face the right way, which effectively eliminates their writing surface.

Please, please take a solemn vow to never, ever, ever-present to an audience while they are eating.

Their attention is split between you and their meal. They need the salt, or the napkin falls on the floor, or the water tips over and makes a mess. The din made by cutlery and china, slurping and chewing strips the presenter of confidence as he/she competes for top billing over the soup and salad. This is a no-win situation to be strenuously avoided.

There are benefits to these seating arrangements as long as food consumption does not occur during the presentation. It is excellent for creating teams and groups for discussions and kinetic learning. As long as the room is not too crowded, safety demands are simple to satisfy. It is friendlier than long rows, and more smiles can be expected. The presenter can define the formality in the room, and as long as his/her room control skills are up to speed, this seating arrangement can be very effective.

Option 5: Boardroom

This arrangement is the standard operating procedure for business presentations. One large table, usually oblong, around which the listeners are seated, and at the head of which stands the presenter.

Option 6: Horseshoe

Similar to this is the horseshoe-shaped table arrangement, chairs along the outside edges, the front of the room and the center of the horseshoe being open to the presenter. It provides excellent sightlines (as long as there are no pillars in the way) where everyone can see everyone else. As you can imagine, having the audience able to observe actions and reactions from the other side of the room can go either way: good if that side of the audience is agreeing with the presenter, not quite as good if someone is engaged in attention-seeking behavior, and catastrophic if someone's body language is loud enough to broadcast a negative reaction to the presenter. The formality of the boardroom dictates appropriate behavior, but a single but loud dissenting attitude can change the atmosphere in the room against the presenter. More on how to handle this kind of situation can be found in the Room Control unit.

Option 7: Office

In business, this is often the first phase of the presentation. It is usually a small meeting held in someone's office, most typically furnished with the owner's desk and chair, a couple of visitor's chairs, maybe a credenza, and perhaps a small round table with a couple of additional chairs. When a presenter is in this space, it is **vital** that there are no physical barriers between the participants and the presenter. Do not speak over a desk; it can lead to intimidation as it gives the advantage to the owner of the desk; sitting beside or adjacent to your counterpart creates a more level playing field. Just as when a presenter speaks from a stage, we open the door to engagement by getting out from behind the lectern, in this situation, we must remove the physical barriers to connection by getting out from behind the desk. Once again, the power spot is the one farthest away from the door, so choose your space wisely.

LIGHTING

If people cannot see you well, they will complain that they cannot hear you. Be mindful that you are not speaking in front of an undraped window. Your face will be in silhouette and when your facial expressions cannot be clearly discerned, it will be much more difficult to create or maintain trust. You may have heard negative references to "shadowy" individuals or those who hide in the "shadows;" keep yourself out of your own shadow!

You may also have heard of actors, "finding their light." Speakers need to find their light, too, and for the same reason; you will not make any meaningful connections, forge powerful relationships, or move any mountains unless you can be seen. If you are working under stage lights, finding the sweet spot is easy; it's where the light in your own eyes is the brightest. If you are working in a boardroom or an office where lighting is uniform, then just don't stand under the one light bulb that isn't working (or even worse, flickering).

SOUND

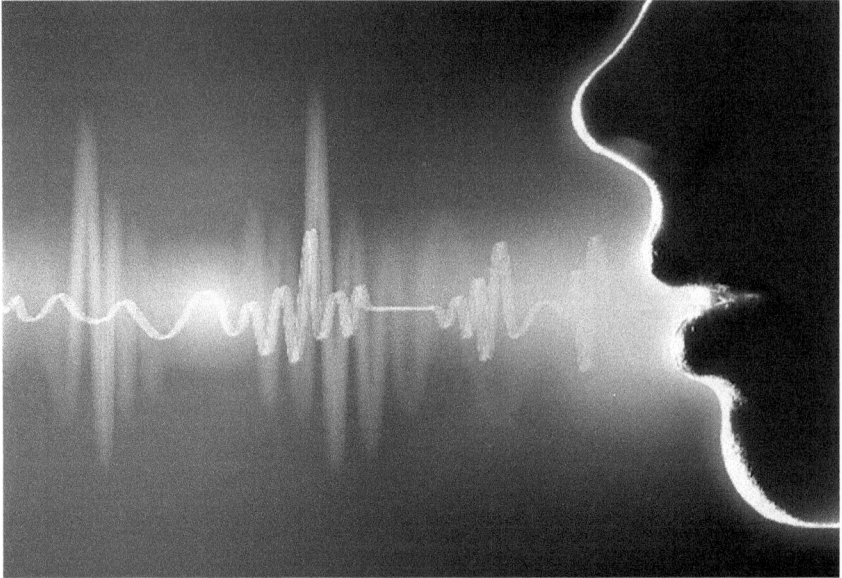

Speakers can go unheard for many reasons.

1. We are not using our voice properly to fill the space, or the sound system is inadequate.
2. Room acoustics have not been properly considered.
3. Ambient noise, like the buzz of fluorescent lighting, external hubbub bleeding into the room, or intercom music acts as a sound buffer between our mouth and their ears.
4. Our facial expressions and body language messages are not aligned with our words which causes confusion; confused minds check out and don't hear anything well.
5. The audience can't see us clearly so they can't lip read, or stay engaged by our gestures, our movement, or our facial

expressions; if they can't see us, they will complain they can't hear us.

6. There is so much wordy information on our slides that the audience tunes us out so they can read it instead. This is covered in more detail in the Enhancements unit.

SPACE LIMITATIONS

Sometimes we find ourselves speaking in spaces that are simply not designed for presentations. The lighting may be too low, the space too crowded, or too large, no clearly defined, "power seat," pillars in the way or a host of other nuisances. When this happens, and it will, it is still up to the speaker to ensure that the listeners get the most possible out of the presentation. Accept the situation, do the best you can to keep your listeners engaged, and do not carp about it or lay blame for it! Be gracious and call on your excellent tool kit of skills to help make your presentation powerful, potent, and persuasive, regardless of the space or its limitations.

CONFIDENT STAGES

Rosemarie Barnes

Chapter 11

Confident Room Control

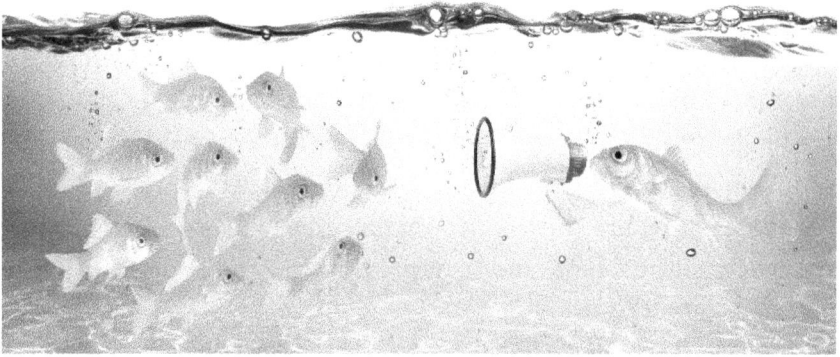

Confident Room Control

From the point of view of the listener, everything about a presentation is ultimately the responsibility of the speaker. While speakers may receive direction from the venue or the event planner, we still need to give thorough consideration to things like seating arrangements, registration and selling tables, breaks, and transitions; the list is large, and the effects of these arrangements, very important. Without effective room control skills, transitions take longer than anticipated and time is never a speaker's friend. Confusion about where to be and when to be there, how long breaks are, or where the washroom facilities are can reflect negatively on the event, and taint previously open and receptive attitudes.

BEFORE

Although discussed in detail in the Use of Space unit, it bears repeating here: if you have control of the seating arrangement in the room, consider the pros and cons of each, both for yourself and on behalf of the audience. Remember that the area farthest away from the main entrance to the room is the place of power. Be careful to not appear in silhouette due to unshaded windows and be aware of pillars or other visual obstructions between you and the listeners. One of the most important considerations is safety; be sure that in case of emergency, everyone can get out quickly.

If you can possibly manage it, greeting people as they enter your room is hugely powerful not only for audience engagement but also for room control. You are greeting them as your guests and inviting them into your room; welcomed guests behave much better than do strangers. If you don't know the names of everyone in your audience, use name tags 1) because you can address them by name as you greet them, and 2) it encourages participation during exercises and activities and is an important first step in building relationships. Using someone's name brings attention to them and makes them feel important and seen. Once you have used someone's name, they subconsciously feel bonded to you like at least an acquaintance, thereby increasing their receptivity to your presentation. There is nothing better for, "warming up the crowd," than to engage in pleasant greetings and a little chitchat, so that when you take to the platform, they view you as approachable, friendly, and warm. Even if they don't like or agree with your presentation, they are more likely to give you the benefit of the doubt, and much less likely to walk out or resort to heckling. If you've gone the extra mile and helped them find a seat, (or had someone else help them) they will consider you to be concerned for their well-being and their receptivity will increase. If you want to make a grand entrance, remove yourself from the room a few minutes before you begin the presentation, and then reappear after you have been introduced.

A quick mention of another selling point of supplying name tags is the benefit of name recognition: yours and between participants. When audience members run into each other at some future date, you will receive free advertising in the form of, "I remember you. Didn't we meet at Rosemarie Barnes' presentation on Bridging the Generations Gaps back in November?" People who have shared names are much more likely to garner recognition of each other. The presentation will create a commonality and a basis for conversation, and you will receive the credit for having brought them together. Be careful that name tags actually stick to clothing or use lanyards, and if you can, brand the tags with your name and logo. You can't buy better advertising.

Registration, Refreshment, Product, and Transaction Tables

If you have registration or product tables, do not attempt to man them yourself. Get help and train your assistants well. Before the presentation, you need time to center yourself and then greet your guests (even with delicate negotiations or controversial topics, your audience are your guests) and your energies are best spent there. If you are offering refreshments, organize them long before the event, and then have someone else take care of it on the day. On that day, your attention must be on providing the best possible value to your guests via your presentation, not by serving coffee and cookies. Ensure that refreshment tables are easily accessible, are organized with traffic flow in mind, and that there are plenty of waste receptacles.

If you are selling products or services, you must consider the best way to display them, where to display them, and the most efficient way of handling transactions. Ensure that hardware for electronic transactions is working, that you have a change float if you accept cash, or if requesting donations, that a beautifully adorned donation receptacle is visible and easily accessible. If you are offering a door prize, consider how and when the winner will be announced.

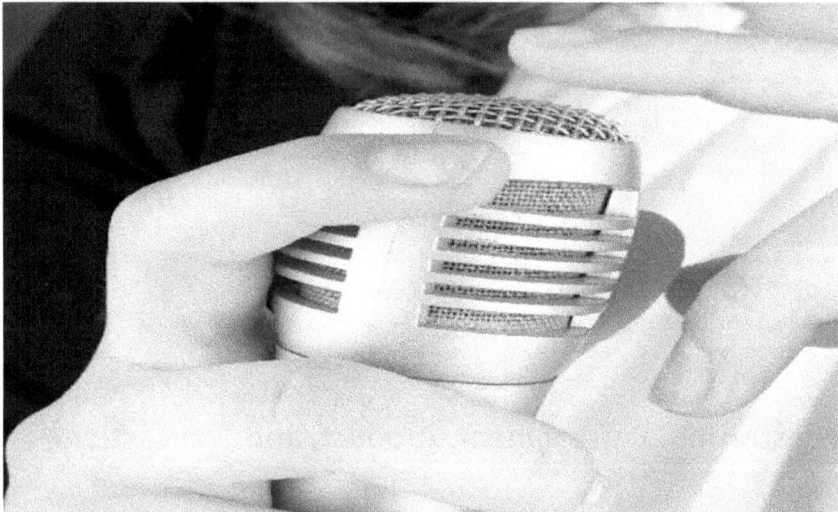

Professionalism is paramount as it garners respect. Can you imagine an emcee at the Academy Awards blowing on the microphone and asking if everyone can hear them? Of course not, yet how often have we seen speakers doing just that? All equipment and sound checks must be done prior to taking to the stage because tapping the microphone to see if it's on makes presenters seem less than in control. When it comes time for the speaker to direct traffic during participatory activities, audiences will pay more attention to the speaker that controls the room.

Letting your audience know your agenda and timetable is a double-edged sword that depends on the reason for and the length of the presentation.

Some presenters believe that by providing their audience with a detailed accounting of what is going to happen and when they are providing structure to the event and sharing responsibility for participation with their listeners.

Others insist that if you give participants an outline of and schedule for the presentation, the speaker is giving away control by allowing listeners the opportunity to opt-out of a piece of the event or plan to check messages during that time. This method of keeping the outline a secret is very popular among speakers whose goal is to sell.

There are pros and cons to both.

DURING

PROGRAMS/AGENDAS/OUTLINES FOR PRESENTATIONS

Supplied Agenda	No Supplied Agenda
Sharing the plan shares responsibility for the benefits of the presentation by allowing listeners to pay more attention to the parts that interest them, and to let their mind wander during other, less tantalizing topics. Where the audience has a vested interest in the outcome of the presentation, supplying a schedule neither enhances nor detracts from the outcome.	No agenda urges the audience to pay constant attention because they don't know what is going to be addressed or when. This method is well used to remove the possibility of pre-selecting or opting out of pieces of the event.
Knowing the schedule allows the audience to plan their calls to the office, to check their messages, and to delay the call of nature until break time. This method reduces disruptive interruptions in favor of organized group breaks.	Because the listeners do not know the schedule, listeners may choose to surreptitiously check messages and take care of their personal needs at times most convenient to themselves. Where the audience has a vested interested in the outcome of the presentation, not supplying a schedule neither enhances nor detracts from the outcome.
More people than not prefer to know what is planned and when it will occur. It provides structure in a structure-based world and creates trust when the speaker fulfills the obligation to follow the plan. Alternately, if the speaker does not follow the agenda exactly as provided, it can cause anxiety thereby reducing attention to the presentation itself.	By encouraging listeners to participate fully in whatever the event brings, many presenters feel they are giving permission to listeners to let the world outside the venue continue to spin without the listener's involvement for the duration of the event. Some individuals welcome the opportunity for complete involvement while others view it as disrespectful to their other obligations.

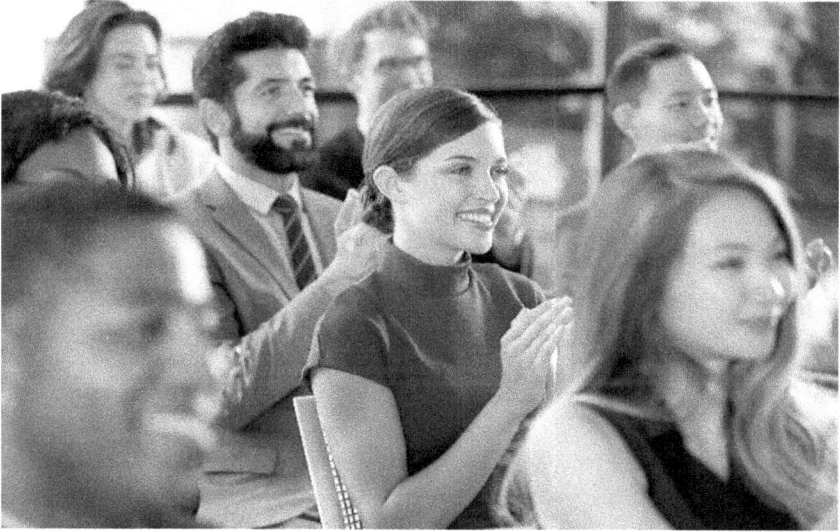

Audience Engagement

There are many tried and true methods of encouraging audience engagement while still maintaining control of the room. Well-known in the world of sales (and ultimately, everyone in business is in sales, and that includes Public Speakers) that physical engagement is powerful. The theory goes that if the audience has been responding to questions by nodding in agreement, or saying, "yes," often, that they will be more comfortable saying, "yes," to purchasing a product or service.

Similarly, having the audience complete speakers' sentences, verbally filling in the blanks as it were, increases engagement. Requesting popcorn callouts ("just call out your answers/suggestions") can lead to chaos, so choose instead to have individuals raise their hands and then call on them for responses. Anything that increases audience engagement improves the likelihood of them accepting your information and then acting on it. That said, the freer the audience engagement, the increased necessity for room and crowd control. This is accomplished by stating parameters, or the rules of the "game" before proceeding with the activity. People will happily play by the rules provided they know what they are; it's the presenter's responsibility to make those rules clear.

Terms of Address

While it is vital that presenters speak the language of the audience, it is equally vital to show respect for them. That means speaking at the more formal end of the accepted language spectrum. If we are addressing an audience of our peers, it is valuable to use commonly accepted phrases and abbreviations such that a bond of understanding is created, but elevate your presentation to the most socially acceptable level of formality. If we are ordering a hamburger at a fast-food outlet, we can accept a more familiar term of address such as, "What can I get you guys today?" If, however, we are at a fine dining establishment where we are paying not only for the food but for the ambiance and service, "What can I get you guys," is far less acceptable. It is always wise to err on the side of a respectful formality than to appear too casual. Our listeners merit respect, that respect being shown via body language, eye contact, and choice of words. With few exceptions, "Ladies and Gentlemen," is far more appropriate than, "You guys," even when addressing children, and will garner much more cooperation as you issue instructions from the speaker's platform.

There is little need to exercise room control once your audience is engaged. It is during periods of transition that things can quiet easily get sidetracked.

Because you are an excellent public speaker, you know that:

-we remember only about 10% of the information we hear,
-we remember about 50% of the things we see, and
-we remember almost all of what we do.

We, therefore, include some sort of experiential opportunity for our listeners to cement the information we provide. It is during the transition periods, into and out of these exercises or experiences, where we must stay in control of the room. Often, audience discussions can become quite animated and decibel levels can increase substantially. Bringing their attention back to you can feel like herding cats or pushing a rope.

Adults do not respond well to be shushed so actively avoid it. Instead, give them a call-back signal before you send them off to group discussions or exercises. Pre-determined callback signals are many and varied. For example:

1. Raise one arm above your head and say nothing. This one works very well because many of us were trained in it during our years as students. It doesn't matter which arm you use as long as it's raised high and straight and I've never seen an audience that doesn't respond to it. The trick is to give it a

bit of time. It may seem to take quite a while for the audience to settle down, but in truth, it is rarely more than 30 seconds; it just feels like an eternity.

2. If the group is small, you can simply announce in a normal presentation voice that it is time to come back, for example, "Please finish your thought and come on back to the group."

3. If the activity or exercise is done individually, you could give time alerts, so participants are not surprised when the time comes to an end. "One more minute to finish up, please," is courteous and clear.

4. If the room has been quiet during the activity, 15 or 20 seconds of music works very well. Ensure that your listeners know beforehand that it is the sign to return their focus to you, and that the music chosen conveys the energy and attitude you want them to absorb.

5. Some presenters use a chime or other attention-getting sound. These can work well depending on the group's demographics and must be chosen wisely because it reflects the personality of the speaker; a light, tinkly chime indicates femininity and right brain thinking, a thunderclap the opposite. Be sure the sound you choose not only reflects your attitude but will be received appropriately by your listeners.

Never, ever try to be heard over the din of energetic audience participation. It indicates a lack of control over the room, and since no one likes to be yelled at, it is rarely received well. A predetermined call-back signal will make the listeners aware of what to listen to, or look for, and the transition will go much faster and smoother.

Always use "please" when calling the group back, and "thank you" once they are settled in again. It indicates respect for their cooperation, which they will mirror back to you.

Breaks

The most generally accepted rule is that after 90 minutes, everyone needs at least a short break. We can push that a little if the presentation has been broken up by frequent participatory opportunities, but even so, 2 hours is the absolute limit before biological needs necessitate interruptions. Always time a break so that the second half is the shorter of the two.

Breaks require clear instructions or 15 minutes will very easily turn into 30 and necessitate changes to the program. Excellent presentations **NEVER go over time**, nor is it acceptable to try and cram 30 minutes of information into a span of only 15. (Review Confident Content if you've forgotten the promise you made right at the beginning of that unit.) If you've done your planning and rehearsal well, you know exactly how long your presentation will take, and your audience will NEVER thank you for going overtime! Keeping breaks on schedule is one of the most important room control skills we have.

Speak to your listeners in the most courteous way about coming back from breaks on time. Remind them that it is to their own benefit and respectful of others to be back in their seats, ready to go, so they can get back to their regular-scheduled lives on time. If you want to give them a quick 10-minute break to go to the washroom or get a glass of water, schedule 15 minutes in your master plan. If the break is for lunch, have your participants inform the restaurant of their schedule immediately after being seated, followed by a request that their bill accompanies their meal so it can be paid without delay. Where the group is sizeable, wherever possible, notify the restaurant to expect an influx of patrons so they can prepare themselves to accommodate your timelines. Once again, give yourself 5 minutes of extra time in the master schedule to allow for stragglers and unforeseen circumstances. Except in the rarest of circumstances, after the break start again at the time you said you would, regardless of whether everyone is back in their seats; it shows respect for those who complied with the timetable and indicates that you are trustworthy and mean what you say.

If refreshments or meals are being catered, be sure dishes and debris are cleared away before continuing your presentation so that attention is focused on you, not the half-eaten bun on the table or the distraction of clinking cutlery. Be sure the caterers know your timeline is firm so they will take steps to satisfy you, their customer.

Questions

Some speakers like to answer questions as they arise, while others prefer to block a time for them. In some situations, it can be beneficial to respond immediately to questions, but It is much easier to maintain the flow of the presentation by allotting a prescribed time for them. The mistake most speakers make (to the point where it is considered normal) is to address questions and comments at the very end of the presentation.

Please don't do that.

We remember the last thing we hear best. Would you rather have your listeners remembering your answer to a question that may a) only pertain to the person asking the question, or b) catch you off-guard and fumbling a little for a reply, or would you rather they remember your powerful closing and call to action?

If you choose to call for questions or comments, the better place to do so is before you launch into your planned closing and inspired call to action. Leave your listeners with your confident voice ringing in their ears and memories by not giving up control of the room. By inserting a question period prior to your close, you can define the amount of time you will give it, by simply saying, "Before we begin the final portion of today's presentation, we can take 5 minutes for questions." Keep track of the time, or better yet, have someone signal you when you have 1-minute left, and then announce that the next question will be the last." Once again, people will play by your rules as long as they know what they are. If time runs out while there are still raised hands and burning question to be addressed, acknowledge that it is so, and offer to answer them later by sharing exactly where you will be and for how long after the presentation is concluded.

"If you have questions or comments, I invite you to address them to me personally. You will find me beside the Grandfather clock in the lobby for 30 minutes after the presentation is over"

When your 30 minutes is up, offer your contact information to those remaining, and suggest they reach out via telephone or electronic call. It will be deemed as fair because you set the parameters beforehand, and your continued willingness to serve, appreciated.

Hecklers

It doesn't happen often, but it can happen. Something you say, the way it was said, or a controversial topic can spark heightened emotions and heated comments. The best way to handle them is to acknowledge the comment, give the individual as much respect as you can muster, (easier to do when you realize you may not fully know what sparked the outburst) and offering to discuss the issue with them privately. Do not enter into an argument with them or demean them in any way. If they continue and refuse to settle down, thank them again for their candor and willingness to share, acknowledge their emotions, and suggest that out of respect for others in the room, that the conversation about the issue would be better done in private and in a calmer state.

"I can see you are upset, and I will do my best to answer your concerns in a private meeting. Come and see me after and we can set up an appointment to do that."

If you continue to take the high road, the heckler will quickly lose the support of the rest of the audience; these kinds of individuals tend to back down when the power of numbers swings against them.

Heckling is rare, especially if speakers come from a place of service, with the intention of giving value, and strive to solve the top-of-mind problems of their audience.

AFTER

Your presentation is not finished until the last participant has left the room and you are on the way home or back to the office. To some degree (like it or not), a presentation is a performance, and a performer's job is not completed just because he/she has no more lines to say. Remember that only 7% of our message is relayed via words, the rest via physiological means, and you are sending messages even when you leave the platform, or take questions under the Grandfather clock, stand with your arms crossed, or use slang language.

Unless the event is very small, get help to sign up clients, sell products, and collect lead generators. Lead generation is discussed in more detail in the "Confident Presentation Impact" unit; suffice to say here that every presentation you give is an opportunity to attract business leads, add to your contact lists, and grow your business, and make no mistake: if you don't treat public speaking as a business it will turn into a very expensive hobby. Make sure you avoid lengthy line-ups at your selling tables; standing in line saps excitement, and ultimately gives potential clients an opportunity to second guess their decision to purchase.

If you are an author and are selling or giving away books, people like to get them signed, so choose a spot for this to happen. You will want a table and a chair at least for yourself and it's a nice touch to make the other person feel important and valued by supplied a seat for them as well. Use a nice pen and have a spare available just in case. Be gracious, and learn to accept compliments with a sincere, "Thank you."

Readily available business cards and clear signage will make the entire AFTER process much more successful.

The day after your presentation still involves your room control skills. Your brilliant lead generators will have provided you with new contacts to pursue and opportunities to investigate. At the very least you will want to thank participants for attending the presentation, or express appreciation for their support. People that assisted you must be rewarded for their efforts, even if it is only an email of thanks. In this day of electronic communications, you might consider sending a thank you card or hand-written note via the good old postal service; it's a nice surprise and shows that you put some effort into showing gratitude. A little graciousness goes a long way, so don't overdo it; but sincere thanks is always appreciated.

CONFIDENT STAGES

Communication Excellence

The mandate for Confident Stages and the Executive Presentation Academy is to provide you with the skills you need to inform, inspire, and invite engagement and participation as you strive to make a difference for yourself and others, and for you to be excellent as you Speak to Engage, Speak to Succeed. I most sincerely hope you have taken value from the Executive Presentation Academy's on-line training programs.

Communication skills are invaluable to the world of business; unfortunately, they are often relegated to the back row of importance, and that comes with hidden and expensive costs. The lack of adequate speaking skills inevitably costs money, loyalty, engagement, and commitment, and can lead to escalating recruitment and retention costs. There is no denying that poorly tuned communication skills are one of the causes of these expenses, and they are substantial. Communication theory and exercises are an excellent way to begin, and the information provided in the Academy's lessons can and will stand you in good stead.

Since we remember only about 10% of what we hear, about 50% of what we see, and almost all of what we do, the pursuit of excellence in communication dictates that in order to fully absorb and internalize learning, experiential opportunities for "doing" must be sought and delivered. Feedback is necessary for growth, that feedback being most valuable when coming from an experienced trainer.

If you will allow me, I would be honored to discuss your unique situation and needs with you and continue to work with you. Because you have already learned much of the theory of excellent communication techniques, you will be given special consideration and price reductions for private or group training.

Rosemarie Barnes

Please accept my invitation for a discovery conversation to explore how I may best serve you and your business in your quest for excellence. You may connect with me on-line at rbarnes@confidentstages.com, via Zoom, or by good old-fashioned telephone at 250 661-0994.

You are also most welcome to join our Facebook community where clients and I meet bi-weekly to mastermind with each other and jointly find solutions to real-time problems. With your permission, your name will be added to our newsletter distribution wherein the goal is to provide nuggets of **Communication Gold**.

I wish you every success in your continuing quest for communication and speaking excellence and am available to provide professional guidance as circumstances dictate.

Rosemarie Barnes

SPECIAL OFFER

Thank you for your dedication and commitment as you worked through the information provided through the recordings and for sharing your questions and concerns during the group video calls. I most sincerely hope you have taken value from your learning and that you experience positive results from your presentations.

To offer consistently excellent presentations takes effort and experience and no two presentations are identical. Even scripted and stock presentations vary in their delivery and impact depending on the speaker's personality, vocal and physical delivery skills, presence, and most importantly, to whom the presentation is addressed. The higher the skill level of the presenter, the more value will be received by the listeners, the higher the level of engagement, followed by more agreement, more action, and increasingly better results.

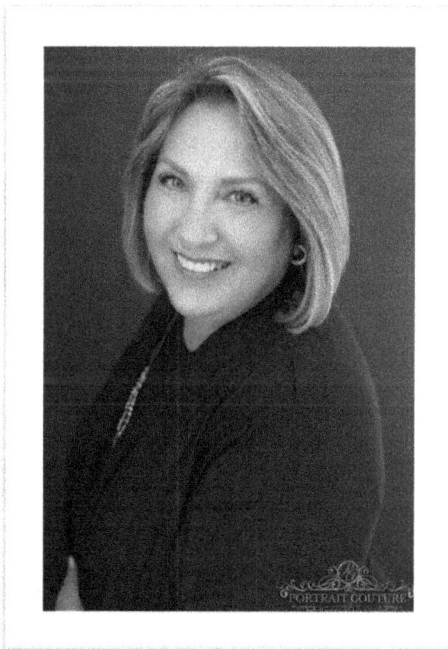

Virtual training is good, group training is good, feedback for growth is good, too, and a tremendous amount of improvement can be realized through these vehicles. When you must be consistently excellent, when the messages you share must be heard, and powerful action taken, you may need a little more. The very best training is done individually with a dedicated trainer. Experientially based and focused on you, one-to-one training can and will make the difference between suggestion and focused inspiration, acceptance and energetic motivation, doubt, and paradigm-shifting action.

You should be rewarded for the work you have already done as you strive to deliver your powerful messages, so it gives me great pleasure to tell you that when you see the benefit of individual attention and detailed training and wish to work with me as your champion for presentation excellence, your individual investment for a 3-month or longer training commitment with me will be reduced by the price of the virtual training you have already completed. If you invested in the Essentials Program, the cost of individual training will be reduced by $450. If it was the Leadership Program, it will be a reduction of $300, and if you took advantage of the Combined Program, that's $600 less for working with me one-to-one, for you, with you, and for your benefit.

All you need to do is have a conversation with me, and we'll set up a program based on what you already know, what you still need to know, and how you learn best.

Continue to strive for excellence for yourself, your business, your teams, and the world. If I can help, it would be my honor to serve you.

Rosemarie Barnes

https://www.confidentstages.com

www.facebook.com/confidentstages

www.ca.linkedin.com/in/rosemarie-barnes

rbarnes@confidentstages.com

www.ingramcontent.com/pod-product-compliance
Lightning Source LLC
Chambersburg PA
CBHW060048100426
42742CB00014B/2733